I'M A GOOD MAN, BUT...

EDITED BY FRITZ RIDENOUR

Featuring Peanuts cartoons by
Charles Schulz

A Division of G/L Publications
Glendale, California, USA

PEANUTS cartoons © United Feature Syndicate, Inc.
1955, 1957, 1958, 1959, 1960, 1961, 1963, 1965, 1967

Scripture quoted from Living New Testament is copyrighted by
Tyndale House Publishers, 1967 and is used by permission.

Excerpts and quotations from books are used by permission
from the publishers.

The publishers do not necessarily endorse the entire
contents of all publications referred to in this book.

Over 100,000 in print
Second Printing, 1969
Third Printing, 1970
Fourth Printing, 1971

© Copyright 1969 G/L Publications

Printed in U.S.A.

Published by
Regal Books Division, G/L Publications
Glendale, California 91209, U.S.A.

Library of Congress Catalog Card No. 75-96702
ISBN 0-8307-0049-8

Contents

A teaching and discussion guide for use with this book is available from your church supplier.

THANK YOU, CHARLIE BROWN AND OTHERS

I'm a Good Man, But . . . is a combination of thoughts from God's Word, thoughts concerning that Word and concepts and ideas and thoughts from the mind of Charles Schulz, world famous creator of the Peanuts Cartoon Strip, which reached its ultimate "height" of fame when "Snoopy" orbited the moon in the spring of 1969.

The purpose behind *I'm a Good Man, But* . . . is to help you grapple with the problem that the title of this book suggests. We all like to believe we are a "good man," *but* life proves us to be something less than that. If we are Christians we have even more cause to think (hope?) that we are good because the Scriptures teach us that the Christian is righteous in God's sight. Again experience (as well as Scripture) convinces us that we don't bat 1.000 in this ball game of life and choosing between good and bad. In fact there are those times when we feel an awful lot like the Charlie Brown who has led his team to glorious defeat 176 to 0. ("How can we lose when we are so sincere?")

I'm a Good Man, But . . . helps you take a look at yourself, your friends and "the authorities" which, for high schoolers (for whom this book is mainly intended) means adults.

Our sincere thanks to Charles Schulz (and his publisher, United Features Syndicate) for graciously allowing us to use "Peanuts" cartoons to help put across key points in each chapter. In our opinion no cartoon of today, or any other day for that matter, speaks more precisely to the human predicament that all of us find ourselves in than "Peanuts."

My thanks, too, to my assistant, Georgiana Walker who played her usual invaluable role as research analyst and who also wrote several of the open-end stories. For other open-end stories appreciation goes to writers Jim Eschenbrenner (Chapter 11), Coleman Coates (Chapter 10) and Marlene Hess (Chapters 6, 7, 8, 9).

We hope those who have done extensive (or even cursory) reading in the field of psychology will be patient with us. We look forward to the time when we might deal with schools of psychological thought and their relationship to the Scriptures.

Fritz Ridenour
Youth Editor
Gospel Light Publications

". . . when the Holy Spirit controls . . . He will produce . . . love, joy, peace . . ." Galatians 5:22

I LOVE MANKIND...BUT

The title of this book comes out of one of the basic "hang-ups" that all of us face. We all want to think we are a "good man" but life just doesn't seem to prove us out.

"You know what your trouble is?" says Lucy to Charlie Brown. "The whole trouble with you is that you're you!"

"Well, what in the world can I do about that?" says Charlie.

"I don't pretend to be able to give advice . . ." says Lucy. "I merely point out the trouble!" (See cartoon, next page.)

It seems that "the trouble" gets pointed out to us rather regularly as we go through life. Some of us do better than others, but all of us face failure, frustration, etc. All of us make mistakes. Our image of a

"good man" gets tarnished by the inevitable soilings that occur. In fact, there are some days when we think we are the "Charlie Brownest" of all.

How do we cope? What if you're a Christian? What does God have to do with it? How can we learn to live more successfully and effectively with ourselves and others? We know we have the desire for good—otherwise we couldn't recognize good from evil. We know that we can love others because we have had moments when it's happened. But our gears seem to be jammed. At least they are grinding a bit from time to time. We "run on all cylinders" for a few minutes, hours, days or even weeks, and then we seem to sputter and miss. And, it seems there are plenty of times when our Christianity—instead of helping us and being a glorious source of

2

power as our pastor assures us each Sunday—seems to get in the way and seems to make it even tougher to be ourselves, to be real and still be a "good man."

For example, one of the key truths that gets pounded into any typical "church kid" from the time he is in cradle roll is "love one another." Now just about anyone (unless he is mentally ill) will agree that "loving one another" is a splendid idea. How this is done is something else again. Many a Christian—young or old—carries a heavy burden of guilt around because he has a consuming hatred (or at least a strong dislike) for a certain person, group, organization, etc. He knows this is wrong, but he doesn't seem to be able to do anything about it. He is in the same boat as Linus who retorts to his sister's claim that he can never become a doctor because he doesn't love mankind by saying, "I love mankind . . . it's people I can't stand!" (See cartoon page 14.)

And then there is the "fruit of the Spirit" which is the subject of many a sermon. "Bearing good fruit" in your life (such as love, joy, peace, etc.) is another idea to which all Christians subscribe, but harvesting this kind of fruit doesn't seem to come easily. Perhaps the problem is that the "fruit of the Spirit" that is mentioned in Gal. 5:22,23 is often held up as some kind of "Mount Everest of Christian attainment" that Christians are supposed to reach frequently, if not daily. Too many Christians see the "fruit of the Spirit" as separate *fruits*—achievements in Christian living. But when you turn the fruit of the Spirit into fruits plural, you commit the typical legalistic religious trap of rules

3

and regulations. Fruits keep eluding you, mocking you and in the end condemning you with guilt feelings because you don't think you are "fruitful enough."

But if you take a careful look at Gal. 5:22,23 you will see that Paul specified something besides rules. He says, "When the Holy Spirit controls our lives He will produce this kind of fruit in us: love, joy, peace, patience, kindness, goodness, faithfulness, gentleness and self-control; and here there is no conflict with Jewish laws" (*Living New Testament*).

Paul's entire purpose in writing the book of Galatians was to help his readers free themselves from the shackles of a "rules and regulations religion." Christianity is not "following a list of rules." It is a relationship to Jesus Christ. When one knows Christ personally, Christ's Holy Spirit is in that person. When the Holy Spirit controls that person's life, then he will see more and more of the elusive and hard to come by fruit—such as love, joy, peace, etc.

Putting the Holy Spirit in complete control is the catch. Charlie Schulz's "Peanuts" characters are good examples of all of us, who want the fruit of the Spirit but who are trapped by our own weakness, greed, pride and selfishness.

For example, Lucy is talking to Charlie Brown and boasting that her family has solidity, loyalty . . . and at that moment Linus comes by dragging his blanket.

"WHY DON'T YOU STOP DRAGGING THAT STUPID BLANKET AROUND, YOU BLOCK-

HEAD!" shouts Lucy at Linus, who does the characteristic "Peanuts flip" from utter shock.

Hardly pausing for breath, Lucy turns to Charlie Brown and continues her boasting by saying, "and love for one another, and. . . ." (See cartoon below.)

Peace is another sought after "pot of gold" at the end of the rainbow for the "Peanuts" characters. Linus, the fearful clutcher of the blanket, probably best exemplifies "man's search for security." In one "Peanuts" adventure we find him at Lucy's psychiatric stand admitting that he's in sad shape; that life is full of fears and anxieties; that all that keeps him going is his blanket. With professional aplomb, Lucy diagnoses his case and encourages him by

telling him that because he realizes that he needs help, he is not yet too far gone. Lucy digs into Linus' psyche, asking him if he has fear of responsibility ("hypengyophobia"); or is it a fear of cats ("ailurophobia"). After mentioning several other phobias, Lucy hits on "pantophobia"—the fear of everything—and Linus shouts "THAT'S IT!" (See cartoon.)

Yes, pantophobia probably is "it" for Linus. He fears everything because he has no peace. When Paul uses the word "peace" in Gal. 5:22, he means having everything of the best, the highest; he means being completely relaxed in the knowledge that your life is in God's hands. The other traits found in the fruit of the Spirit—patience, kindness, goodness, etc.—are all illustrated in reverse by the "Peanuts" clan. Patience seems to be produced in the fewest amounts by the Tigress of the "Peanuts" family—Lucy, fastest fist on the block. One of the predominant themes in the "Peanuts" cartoon strip is amusing but still appalling: unkindness of the "Peanuts" kids toward Charlie Brown. "Faithfulness" is another favorite Schulz theme, usually illustrated through Snoopy, the wonder dog, who is not a dog at all but possibly the most "human" of all the "Peanuts" characters.

"Gentleness" (or lack of same) is illustrated best by the impatient Lucy who usually comes on as soft as a bulldozer. But she often meets her match in Snoopy, who has learned the Biblical lesson in Prov. 15:1: "A soft answer turns away wrath." In one "Peanuts" episode, Charlie Brown wants Snoopy to stay away from Lucy's house because she's

6

PSYCHIATRIC HELP 5¢

THE DOCTOR IS IN

I'M IN SAD SHAPE!

MY LIFE IS FULL OF FEAR AND ANXIETY.. THE ONLY THING THAT KEEPS ME GOING IS THIS BLANKET...I NEED HELP!

WELL, AS THEY SAY ON T.V., THE MERE FACT THAT YOU REALIZE YOU NEED HELP, INDICATES THAT YOU ARE NOT TOO FAR GONE...

I THINK WE HAD BETTER TRY TO PINPOINT YOUR FEARS...IF WE CAN FIND OUT WHAT IT IS YOU'RE AFRAID OF, WE CAN LABEL IT...

ARE YOU AFRAID OF RESPONSIBILITY? IF YOU ARE, THEN YOU HAVE HYPENGYOPHOBIA!

I DON'T THINK THAT'S QUITE IT..

HOW ABOUT CATS? IF YOU'RE AFRAID OF CATS, YOU HAVE AILUROPHOBIA

WELL, SORT OF.. BUT I'M NOT SURE...

ARE YOU AFRAID OF STAIRCASES? IF YOU ARE, THEN YOU HAVE CLIMACOPHOBIA

MAYBE YOU HAVE THALASSOPHOBIA..THIS IS A FEAR OF THE OCEAN, OR GEPHYROPHOBIA, WHICH IS A FEAR OF CROSSING BRIDGES...

OR MAYBE YOU HAVE PANTOPHOBIA.. DO YOU THINK YOU MIGHT HAVE PANTOPHOBIA?

WHAT'S PANTOPHOBIA?

THE FEAR OF EVERYTHING..

THAT'S IT!!!

SCHULZ

7

having a "crab-in." Undaunted, Snoopy knocks on the door and when Lucy peers out he gives her a big kiss smack on the nose. Then Snoopy walks away leaving a stunned and docile Lucy on the porch. Snoopy's final observation: "That's how you break up a crab-in."

But Snoopy does have his problems with self-control. Another much desired trait which we wish we could see in our lives. A classic "Peanuts" cartoon shows Charlie Brown fixing two bowls of dog food for Snoopy's supper. As he serves Snoopy his supper, he tells him that he will be gone all day tomorrow and so he has brought an extra bowl of food. Charlie's advice is not to get greedy and to save the extra bowl until tomorrow.

The next several scenes show Snoopy in his classic pose—lying on top of his doghouse—with one bowl of food still on the ground. Snoopy begins to sweat. He begins to grimace. Finally he can stand it no longer. He leaps from the doghouse roof with a mighty snarl and gobbles up the bowl of food. His final comment: 'I'm glad I ate it. I would have hated myself if tomorrow never came!"

We all identify with Snoopy here. We've all faced temptations where we've tried to exercise self-control but we just had to take that extra piece of cake. We had to stay up and watch the late-late show, even though we had a big English quiz in first period the next day. We had to get that additional record—we just *had* to do so many different things because we couldn't control our greed and self-indulgence.

Perhaps it's greed, self-indulgence and selfishness

that really stand between us and the fruit of the Spirit.

Is there any hope for change? Can we become the "good man" that God wants us to be? This book is designed to give you some "live options." It points you to the Scriptures, but it also gives you opportunity to do your own thinking. Hopefully, when you are through with this book, you will have one basic conclusion in mind: "God can and will overhaul my life—if I let Him."

CHAPTER 2

" 'You must love others as much as yourself' " Mark 12:31

DO I
LIKE ME?

Ever ask yourself that question? Maybe your problem is that you already know the answer so you haven't bothered to ask. A lot of people don't like themselves. The result is that they don't like anybody else either, and nobody seems to like them.

In order to "like yourself" you have to have some kind of feeling that you are at least somebody. But a lot of people feel that they are nobody. A lot of us seem as helpless as Linus in the cartoon on page 11. A lot of us feel like screaming sometimes, "If anyone is a someone, I am!!!"

Ironically enough, being a Christian—or at least a subscriber to the claims of Christianity and a member of the local church—doesn't always seem to help either. The Scriptures promise us life more abundantly. We are admonished to take our burdens to Christ. But somehow the positive points of Christianity have been lost in the shuffle and we don't gain the real benefits that Jesus offers. And all too many Christians don't even feel that it's right to think well of yourself. After all, isn't Christianity a matter of "crucifying the flesh"? Isn't a good Chris-

tian a person who is humble, self-effacing, always taking a back seat, going the second mile, turning the other cheek and in general being an all-American doormat?

So, it's no wonder that if you ask some Christians "Do you like yourself?" they answer, "Why no. I'm not supposed to, am I?" But is that really what Jesus said? There's an easy way to find out. Just keep reading. . . .

Can you love your neighbor and hate yourself?

"One of the teachers of religion who was standing there listening to the discussion realized that Jesus had answered well. So he asked, 'Of all the commandments, which is the most important?' Jesus replied, 'The one that says, "Hear, O Israel! The Lord our God is the one and only God. And you must love Him with all your heart and soul and mind and strength." The second is: "You must love others as much as yourself." No other commandments are greater than these.' The teacher of religion replied, 'Sir, You have spoken a true word in saying that there is only one God and no other. And I know it is far more important to love Him with all my heart and understanding and strength, and to love others as myself, than to offer all kinds of sacrifices on the altar of the Temple.' Realizing this man's understanding, Jesus said to him, 'You are not far from the Kingdom of God.' And after that, no one dared ask Him any more questions" (Mark 12:28–34—*Living New Testament, Paraphrased*).

The "Third Great Commandment . . ."

Interesting, isn't it, that when Christ uttered His "summary of all the law" in two great commandments, He taught us that we should love God, love others, and love *ourselves*. Interesting, too, is that psychology is in basic agreement with this Biblical teaching. Psychologists and psychiatrists are constantly working with people who do not love themselves and therefore have no capacity to love others. If you do not love yourself (think of yourself as a God planned individual, having certain worth and value) you cannot love others. Self-love and love of others are not opposites. They exist together or neither one exists at all.

Behind this idea of loving yourself, and loving others as much as yourself are some basic Scriptural principles . . .

You are created by God in His own image and so is every other person. That means you are special, and everyone else is special, too.

God loves you. The Bible says God loves the world, not just the "good people." This is what John 3:16 (that favorite Sunday school memory verse) is talking about: "For God loved the world so much that He gave His only Son so that anyone who believes in Him shall not perish but have eternal life" (*Living New Testament*).

God loves you just as you are. There are no strings, no "qualifications" to be loved by God. God could care less about how much money you've got, what color you are, how popular you are, what you look like, if you're nice or nasty, etc. As Peter discovered one day, "I see very clearly that the Jews are not God's only favorites!" (See Acts 10:34, *Living New Testament*). No, the Jews aren't God's only favorites, although some of them got a funny idea they were and part of the reason that God had to send Christ to die for man's sins was to straighten out this very human tendency to think that "some of us are better than others."

What Jesus is saying when He gives the "two great commandments" is that because God loves you and has communicated with you, you have the opportunity to respond to Him and love Him back. And that's the first commandment—to love God with all your heart, mind, soul and body. The second one says love your neighbor, and right behind it comes what might be called "the third great commandment"—love yourself. That just isn't tacked on to sound spiritual. Loving yourself is really the secret of loving your neighbor. And loving God (and knowing He loves you) is really the secret to loving yourself!

Apparently, Linus hasn't learned this truth yet—at least in the cartoon on page 14. Behind Linus' feeling that he can't stand people is the basic feeling that he can't stand himself.

Knowing that you are a "somebody" because God made you . . . knowing that you are worth something because God has put a price on you that is far higher than even the national debt . . . knowing that God loves you and that you can love Him . . . and knowing that because you love God you can love yourself and others . . . all these things are part of finding out who you really are.

The reason a lot of people get fouled up in this life is that they don't really know who they are. They have no real convictions, they have no real standards, they have no real concept of what their lives are supposed to mean. All of us face pressures, frustrations, failures, defeats, that make us wonder if we're worth very much or if anyone cares. It's hard to like yourself if you don't think anybody else likes you either. This might have been Ralph's problem. Ralph is a "fictitious character," but perhaps, here and there, his story will give you glimpses of yourself. You may or may not have had (or be having) trouble with drugs. But drugs are definitely a part of the scene today, and drugs are lousing up a lot of lives—a lot of lives being lived by people who don't love themselves and don't think anyone else does either.

This story on Ralph is "open-end"—meaning that you sort of put yourself in his place and supply the ending as you would call the shots. You are to put yourself in Ralph's place as you decide . . .

At the Crossroads or Past?

"C'mon, try one. It's not habit forming—not as habit forming as the beer we've been drinking. It'll really turn you on."

Ralph couldn't help but recoil just a little bit as Jack thrust the marijuana cigarette his way.

"Whatsa matter? Do you think your Sunday school teacher will find out?"

"My Sunday school teacher?" thought Ralph. "That's a laugh. I haven't been to Sunday school often enough during the last year to even know who my Sunday school teacher is."

As Ralph thought back over the past few months he realized he hadn't spent much time with anyone but Jack and Jack's friends. And now it was Jack who was trying to get him to try pot.

Ralph thought of his parents. Every week they tried to get him to go to church and Sunday school with them. Until last year he had gone—for as long as he could remember. But now he usually had something else planned for Sunday. Why go? The church was halfway across town and none of the kids at Ralph's school went there. For a long time, Ralph had one special church friend, but after he moved away Ralph felt left out of things. The church "clique"—as he called the kids who sort of ran the church group—all went to Franklin High and were always talking about what had happened at their school, or something that was going to happen. "Unfriendly" was the way Ralph described them.

Ralph tried to get his parents to understand that

the new guys he'd met at school were really friendly and they had plenty on the ball. Especially Jack—a junior—who already had one year of high school under his belt and was sure he knew how to handle just about any situation. Just last week Ralph had told his dad, "Those fellows I go around with at school are real friends. I'm even trying to witness to Jack. He'd do anything for me."

The part about witnessing to Jack was true. Once Ralph had tried to tell Jack about making a "decision to be a Christian" at summer church camp. But Jack put him down in a hurry saying, "I don't need a crutch called God, and you don't either. I never did meet any church guys who were really sharp. What do those fellows over at your church do for you?"

"What does anyone do for me?" was Ralph's big question. "Or, to be more exact, who wants to do anything for me. Or let's face it, am I worth doing anything for?" Ralph's mixed up questions kept racing around in the same old circles they'd been going in for the past months.

The trouble was, Ralph couldn't seem to come up with any answers. And what was worse, no one heard his questions. His dad was seldom at home except on weekends—an executive job kept him away early and late. His mom gave him lots of advice and good food, but she certainly didn't understand how he felt. And going back to the "decision for Christ" Ralph had made at camp—he actually had meant it at camp when he said he wanted to be a Christian, but somehow he'd never understood what it really meant to be one.

And on top of things not going too well at home or at church, school was loused up, too. Try as he would, Ralph felt that everyone else knew the score better than he did. "I thought maybe wanting to do something about God would help," thought Ralph. "But I'm still in a mess. I hate myself. Seems like the only time I'm on top of things is when I'm out with Jack and the fellows and we've had a beer or two."

And so, here they were—in Jack's car, parked at one of their favorite beer drinking spots and for the first time Jack was offering the boys some marijuana.

"I got the joints from my brother," Jack explained. "He's been trying pot and even LSD at college. He's at home this weekend and I talked him into giving these to me."

Ralph looked long and hard at the funny looking little cigarette that was twisted shut at both ends. Jack had already lit one, and the sweet sticky smell of marijuana was already going through the car. The other guys were lighting theirs.

"C'mon, Ralph," urged Jack with a little irritation in his voice. "There's nothing to worry about. It will make you feel great. My brother says that pot can't hurt you and it won't be long until the stuff's legal."

What should Ralph do?

As you think about Ralph's problem, compare his attitudes and feelings with what Jesus says earlier in this chapter about loving God, your neighbor and yourself. Would you say that Ralph loves himself? How does Ralph see himself? How does he see God? Ralph seems to be aware of laws and rules. He even seems to be trying to love his "neighbor" (Jack and his other "buddies"). But Ralph seems a little fuzzy on this business of loving God. Why is he fuzzy? Are you fuzzy on this? Why?

Ralph claims that he sincerely wants to be a Christian. He is not sure he "really accepted Christ" and now things seem to be all muddied up. Do you think Ralph is sincere, or is he really being phony? Is Ralph in a position—with that marijuana cigarette staring him in the face—to make a decision that would really clear up the muddy water quite a bit? What decision would that be?

Can Ralph refuse the marijuana cigarette and still keep Jack and the other guys as buddies? Or should Ralph "go along" and smoke one stick of pot in order to show Jack and the others that he is "no square"? How do the two great commandments fit in here? Many drug users claim that their particular method of turning on helps them to love God all the more. Do you agree? Do you think that in this case smoking marijuana would help Ralph to love God more? Is loving God really Ralph's main concern? What is Ralph's main concern?

Coming back to a question asked a little earlier, is Ralph to the point where he could make a decision that would really clear things up quite a bit? As the title of the "open-end" story asks, is he at the crossroads or past them? After all, he has been drinking beer with Jack and the other boys. He has quit going to church. Is he a spiritual dropout? Is he a total loss in God's scorebook?

What can you do?

These ten questions won't give you a total picture, but you will get a few more clues that can help you wrestle with this idea of loving your neighbor as yourself.

PERSONAL PROFILE TEST

	DEFI-NITELY!	PROB-ABLY	NEUTRAL	UNLIKELY	NEVER!
1. I am terribly hurt if someone criticizes me or scolds me.	___	___	___	___	___
2. I find it hard to talk when I meet new people.	___	___	___	___	___
3. I often feel lonely.	___	___	___	___	___
4. I don't like to contribute to discussions in class at school.	___	___	___	___	___
5. I doubt if I will be as successful as most people.	___	___	___	___	___
6. I am deeply concerned when someone has a poor opinion about me.	___	___	___	___	___
7. I do not want a job that demands a lot of competition.	___	___	___	___	___
8. I tend to be a rather shy person.	___	___	___	___	___
9. I tend to daydream a lot.	___	___	___	___	___
10. I am eager to get along with others.	___	___	___	___	___

This profile test, designed by Larry Richards, is based on research done by Morris Rosenberg, sociologist, and it can serve as an indicator to the way you feel about yourself. "If your check marks fell mostly to the left of the center column (the one labeled "neutral"), down deep (inside), you probably have a low estimate of yourself." In other words, you have low self-esteem. The farther to the left your answers point, the stronger is this feeling of low self-esteem. You probably tend to downgrade yourself, and you are probably smarter, better looking, and more able than you think you are. In short, says Richards, you probably tend to undervalue yourself and your talents.

"If your checks lie to the right of the center column," Richards says that "deep down you have a positive picture of yourself. You . . . see yourself as someone who is worthwhile, with something positive to contribute to life and to others. Your self-esteem is higher."

Of the two conditions—low self-esteem or high self-esteem—obviously, "it is better to feel good about yourself than to feel bad." This may seem foreign to your thinking and to some of the Bible teaching that you have been hearing throughout your life, which condemns pride, self-love and conceit. But to feel good about yourself is not necessarily to be overly-proud, self-centered or conceited. To feel good about yourself is to see yourself as you really are including all the faults, all the chips, scratches and imperfections in yourself and to accept it because you know that in God's sight you're a person of value and with the help of His Spirit, you can become the person He planned for you to be. Once you can do that, you can go on to accepting and loving others and contributing to life as you know it.

Author Richards says that it is better to feel good about yourself because: "Life isn't static. We don't get stranded on a broken treadmill. Life is moving; we're moving. We'll each be different, for better or for worse, next week, next month, next year. But the person who feels negatively about himself is less likely to see the future as an adventure and an opportunity. He's apt to drag his feet. His feelings about himself can weigh him down, hold him back, and stunt his growth toward reality."*

*Are You for Real?, Larry Richards. Copyright 1968, Moody Bible Institute, Moody Press, pp. 52-54.

Drug use and abuse

Drug use and abuse has made headlines for the last few years. Where do you stand on this question of drugs? Check one of the following statements which most closely represents your point of view:

____1. Drugs are definitely bad news and I have no desire whatsoever to be mixed up with them.

____2. There seems to be a lot of pro and con information on drugs. I would like to know more about it.

____3. I see nothing wrong with using drugs if you are careful.

Write down your own feelings on the following question: "For the Christian, drugs are permissible/taboo because . . ."

To help you think through this business of just who you really are, write on the following question or discuss it with a friend: "Who Am I?"

CHAPTER 3

"Don't you realize that you can choose your own master?"
Romans 6:16

BUT I
JUST WASN'T
MYSELF

Ever hear someone say that? Ever make that kind
of apology yourself? When someone says "But I just
wasn't myself!" you are hearing an interesting statement. Behind it is the idea that: (a) "I'm not happy
with something I said or did"; (b) "I just 'know' I
wouldn't have fouled things up so badly if I could
have just been my normal, sweet, capable, intelligent self."

But is "being yourself" really the whole answer?
What do we mean when we say this? Who are we
really? What kind of attitudes do we bring to situations that put us "under the gun"—those minor to
major crises that threaten, frustrate, or even hurt
us?

YOU PROMISED ME A BIRTHDAY PARTY, AND NOW YOU SAY I CAN'T HAVE ONE! IT'S NOT FAIR!

YOU'RE NOT USING THE RIGHT STRATEGY

WHAT?

THE MORE YOU FUSS, THE WORSE OFF YOU'LL BE...WHY NOT ADMIT IT WAS ALL YOUR OWN FAULT?

WHY NOT GO UP TO MOM, AND SAY TO HER, "I'M SORRY, DEAR MOTHER...I ADMIT I'VE BEEN BAD, AND YOU WERE RIGHT TO CANCEL MY PARTY...FROM NOW ON, I SHALL TRY TO BE GOOD"

THAT'S MUCH BETTER THAN RANTING AND RAVING...ALL THAT DOES IS PROVE HER POINT

"I'M SORRY, DEAR MOTHER, I ADMIT I'VE BEEN BAD, AND YOU WERE RIGHT TO CANCEL MY PARTY"...FROM NOW ON, I SHALL TRY TO BE GOOD!"

I'D RATHER DIE!

SCHULZ

Are we often like Lucy in the cartoon on the previous page? There is a "solution" to Lucy's problem. It's even a clever and practical way out, when you think about it. But Lucy's pride is at stake. Give in? Buckle under to the establishment (mother)? She'd rather die!

Put yourself in Lucy's place and just for conversation, suppose that you are a Christian (or at least trying to act like one). When Lucy says "I'd rather die!" she makes a basic choice. Not between living and dying, but between pride (sin) and constructively loving (righteousness). Now it is obvious that Lucy has made the wrong choice. We all identify with her, however, because we've all clenched our fists, gritted our teeth, and said the same thing on occasion.

But this brings up an interesting question. Suppose the Christian faces a "fiery trial" of some kind and winds up saying "Give in? Apologize? Not me—I'd rather die!" Does this mean that he's not really saved? Because he chooses the obstinate, stubborn, unloving way, does this mean that he is a phony or that God is asleep at the switch? Not exactly. Being a Christian doesn't recast you immediately in "instant perfection plastic." Some people experience rapid change and almost "overnight improvement" when they believe; others change and grow more slowly (and some don't grow at all for a while and suddenly make real progress).

The point, however, is that being a Christian means you turn yourself and your sin over to Christ. What being a Christian does do is *put you in a position to choose a better way.* Before you became a

Christian, you see, you had no choice. You could only choose sin. In fact, you were a slave to sin. Before coming to Christ, every person's "real self" is hung up with sin. After coming to Christ, your "real self" is what Christ wants you to be and become. But this isn't always easy. He seldom does it for you overnight. It's usually a process of change and growth. How does it work? Read on . . .

Up from slavery to slavery

"Should we keep on sinning when we don't have to? For sin's power over us was broken when we became Christians and were baptized to become a part of Jesus Christ; through His death the power of your sinful nature was shattered.

"So look upon your old sin nature as dead and unresponsive to sin, and instead be alive to God, alert to Him, through Jesus Christ our Lord. Do not let sin control your puny body any longer; do not give in to its sinful desires. Do not let any part of your bodies become tools of wickedness, to be used for sinning; but give yourselves completely to God—every part of you—for you are back from death and you want to be tools in the hands of God, to be used for His good purposes. Sin need never again be your master, for now you are no longer tied to the law where sin enslaves you, but you are free under God's favor and mercy.

"Does this mean that now we can go ahead and sin and not worry about it? (For our salvation does not depend on keeping the law, but on receiving God's grace!) Of course not! Don't you realize that you can choose your own master? You can choose sin (with death) or else obedience (with acquittal). The one to whom you offer yourself—he will take you and be your master and you will be his slave. Thank God that though you once chose to be slaves of sin, now you have obeyed with all your heart the teaching to which God has committed you. And now you are free from your old master, sin; and you have become slaves to your new master, right- eousness. I speak this way, using the illustration of slaves and masters, because it is easy to understand: just as you used to be slaves to all kinds of sin, so now you must let yourselves be slaves to all that is right and holy. In those days when you were slaves of sin you didn't bother much with goodness. And what was the result? Evidently not good, since you are ashamed now even to think about those things you used to do, for all of them end in eternal doom. But now you are free from the power of sin and are slaves of God, and His benefits to you include holiness and everlasting life. For the wages of sin is death, but the free gift of God is eternal life through Jesus Christ our Lord" (Rom. 6:2,3,11-23, *Living New Testament, Paraphrased*).

Which dog do YOU feed the most?

Romans 6 isn't exactly the easiest passage of the Bible to understand. All this talk about slaves sounds rather alien to 20th century ears. But Paul was writing to Christians in Rome in A.D. 57. And that's why he uses the illustration of slaves and masters. He knows it will be easy for his original readers to understand.

In order to make it easier for us to understand some 19 centuries later, we need to know that slav- ery was common in first century Rome. In fact, there were more slaves in Roman society than there were "free men." When you were a slave, you were completely owned by your master. Your master had the power of life and death over you. And, unless you were purchased by someone else, you remained the property of your master for life.

So Paul is telling the Roman Christians that before they were Christians they were slaves to a master called sin. They had no other choice. They had no other option. Because they had been born in sin, they could serve no other master as far as living their lives was concerned. But when they believed in Christ and became Christians, they were freed from their old master. Indeed, Christ paid the price to set them free. This is the meaning of that Biblical term called "redemption." And, they became slaves to a new master—Jesus Christ.

So the point Paul is making here is that as far as God is concerned, the Christian has a completely new set of options regarding his behavior. He can come into a situation that is frustrating, threatening or painful, and he can choose what he wants to do. His new master—righteousness through Christ Himself—doesn't hold him with any kind of chains. Instead he is "bound by love." Ironically, he is God's slave, but he is free to choose what he wants to do. This is the only way that God could really work it out because if God did anything else He would have to become a Simon Legree or a computer programmer. And so, the Christian can choose which "master" he wants to obey. He can go back to his old master—sin. He can grit his teeth, clench his fists, and shout "I'd rather die!" But when the Christian makes the choice to "rather die" than give in, apologize, do what he knows is right, etc., he is only choosing to follow the old master he was trying to get rid of in the first place—the sin, the hang-ups, the basic moral weak spot that he admitted when he came to Christ.

On the other hand, because he knows God through Christ, the Christian has potential and power (if he chooses to use that power) *to make a different choice*. Admittedly, making this other choice (to give in, to apologize, to do what you know is right) is not easy. Our basic human nature screams that we would "rather die" than humble ourselves or admit we were wrong. But that's what Christianity is all about.

Christianity is turning us from the wrong to the right. And as the Christian yields himself inch by inch to Christ's love, he becomes the real person that God wants him to be. When the Christian fouls up the detail and then apologizes by saying, "I'm sorry. I just wasn't myself," he was never so right. He isn't the self that God knows he can be, and that's what the process of being a Christian is all about.

A supposedly true story from the mission field pretty well sums it up. The missionary was talking to the old Indian about what it was like to be a Christian and the Indian said that being a Christian was like having two dogs inside of him fighting. There was the bad dog (sin) and the good dog (righteousness).

"Which is winning?" asked the missionary.

"The one I feed the most."

There you have it. Which dog are you feeding the most? Many of us seem to keep both dogs quite fat, but hopefully the good dog will eventually win out. Hopefully we will feed the good dog a little more with each passing day and week and year. That's what the mouthful called "sanctification" means. Becoming "sanctified"—more and more like Christ because you are set apart by God for His service—is not a state of perfection. It is not a goal at which you arrive when you make that basic decision to "accept Christ." Christian sanctification—living out the Christian life—is a way of traveling with God through life. And becoming sanctified is a matter of making daily choices with the help of God's Holy Spirit. We make thousands of choices each day—to get up; to speak, not to speak; to be on time, to be late; to be kind, to be mean; left turn, right turn; speed up, slow down; eat; watch TV; read a book; call a friend; etc., etc., etc. A lot of these choices, believe it or not, take the Christian further away or place him closer to the person God intends him to be. It all depends on which "dog" he is feeding the most.

The following "open-end" story describes a girl you may be able to identify with quite easily. At least, you undoubtedly know someone who is a lot like this. As you hear Janie describe herself and her current problem, analyze the attitudes that she is bringing to decision-making situations. How is she coming at this business of making choices? Which dog is she feeding the most?

If Only They'd Let Me Alone!

"I'm Janie. Sure, I'm a Christian. In fact, I'm the social chairman of our youth group at church. I even go with the youth team that goes down to the mission a couple of times each month and I play the piano when they have Sunday afternoon Sunday school for the little kids that live near the mission. But I guess you'd say I'm a messed-up Christian. I've got a real problem. I've got an absolutely terrible temper that's always getting me into trouble.

"Like Friday . . . at gym. My teacher knew that I hurt my foot in class the day before so I told her that I wasn't going to dress since I couldn't play. But she said that I'd better dress. I told her that it was senseless when all I could do was to sit and watch. She got so unreasonable that I really blew my top. I told her how stupid it was the way teachers always think they can push kids around. And, well . . . I ended up in the counsellor's office. The worst part about it is that this isn't the first time this year the same kind of thing has happened. And every time I ask myself the same question: How do I get myself into such messes? Really, that's not the kind of person I am.

"If only people would let me alone and not always pick on me. If only I could just be myself. When I blow up I'm not me at all. Adults are such creeps—they always think about what they want you to do. They never listen. I'd just like to get away from all this for a while. Maybe the kids who cop out on pills aren't so stupid after all. At least they get away from the pressure for a few hours.

"I don't even want to go to school tomorrow . . . the counsellor says I have to apologize to my gym teacher to get back into class. Talk about impossible situations . . ."

What should Janie do?

Janie calls her situation "impossible." Do you agree? Why or why not? What does the Christian do in "impossible situations"?

What connection do you see between Janie's problem and the apostle Paul's statements about choosing the master you want to obey—God or sin? Janie is obviously an "active Christian." But is she aware of the real choices that are hers as a Christian? Would Romans 6:15–23 give her any help?

When Janie says "I'm not myself when I blow my top," what is she really saying? Do you think that she has discovered her "real self"—the self that she can be as a Christian? For example, is there any other option for Janie to choose as far as "holding her temper" is concerned? What option is that? The Bible teaches that the Christian can "do all things through Christ" (Phil. 4:13). Do you think that a Christian can "hold his bad temper" through Christ? Exactly how does the Christian go about doing this? Is it "black magic" and does the Christian just turn himself over to God's automatic controls or is there something else involved, and if so, what?

WHAT CAN YOU DO?

Study the following diagram* and see just how Janie in the hypothetical open-end story, "If Only They'd Let Me Alone!" fits in. Then think about yourself and see if this diagram applies to you also.

*From *Are You for Real?*, Larry Richards, p. 43.

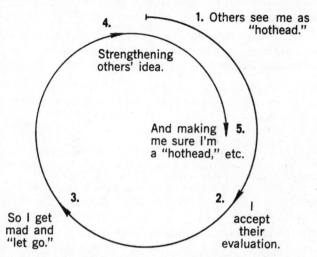

Maybe you identify with Janie quite well, or maybe being a "hothead" isn't your problem at all. But what is your particular hang-up? Perhaps you could fill in the word shy, cold, aggressive, dull or some other attitude instead of the word "hothead." The important thing is to think carefully about just how this vicious circle can build wrong ideas in our minds about ourselves. The key is in point 2, accepting the evaluation of what others see in us. There is no law that says that we have to accept anyone's evaluation of us. The only evaluation we accept is God's evaluation, and He is seeing us with the 20–20 eyes of perfection. In his book *Are You for Real?* author Larry Richards points out that the pictures that other people have of us are the pictures that they want to have for certain reasons known only to them. For example, the mother of an unwanted child often reflects a picture that tells that child "You are unlovely. Unwanted. A burden." Or a father drives his son to make him the athlete that the father never was. Unfortunately the boy doesn't become a star, and so the father labels him a failure and the boy accepts that evaluation and decides that he can never succeed in anything in life. Richards says, "Pictures like these are distorted. To God (and ultimately His evaluation is the one that counts) each of us is of infinite worth. Christ cared enough to die for us. Each has a unique place in God's plan. . . . The Christian is someone who 'in his own special way' can help others so that we will all be healthy and growing and full of love (see Eph. 4:16). There need be no 'failures.' There is a purpose in your life, a place only you can fill."[*]

Try writing down a brief description of yourself as you believe your parents would give it, as your best friend would give it, as one of your teachers would give it. Are these evaluations all the same? Do these evaluations fit what you really believe you are?

Next, write down some specific changes you can make in your habits and your behavior to give people a better image of yourself and thus confirm what you feel is the real image that you want to project because you know Christ.

*Are You for Real?, Larry Richards, p. 43,44.

CHAPTER 4

"You are living a brand new kind of life . . ."
Colossians 3:10

BUT I DON'T SEEM TO CHANGE A BIT!

A change for the better . . . that's what they promise you, and that's what you expect. You accept Christ and you are to become a new creature . . . you go from darkness to light . . . peace of mind and power for living . . . sounds great! But . . . for a lot of Christians it never quite seems to "come off."

Then, too, if you have grown up in the church there has probably been little or no dramatic change. There was no "moment of truth" when you gave up "the bottle," "the needle," or your "life of crime," etc., to become a child of God. It seems that you've "always been a Christian." You've always been law abiding, trying to keep your nose clean, but it all doesn't seem to mean much. You can't recall any real changes, but you have to admit that you have plenty of hang-ups.

Remember "Which dog do you feed the most?" in the last chapter? It's only a story, but it makes a point. For the Christian, there *is* a battle going on inside. We know what Lucy is talking about when,

in a "Peanuts" cartoon, she draws a heart half black and half white and tells Linus that "There are two forces constantly at war with each other in the human heart." And you know exactly how Linus feels as he grabs his middle and gulps "I can feel them fighting." (See cartoon above.)

So, what gives? Is Christianity a phony bill of goods? Is God a cop-out? Well, this problem of "not enough change" has been going on for quite a while. In fact, the first generation of Christians—the first century—had plenty of trouble. There was, for example, this Christian church over in what is now Turkey, in a town known as Colossae at that time. Paul the apostle wrote to them about change, about matching behavior with profession. And, he got right down to the nitty-gritty—to the basic question a lot of us forget or ignore: "Is this whole thing called Christianity a matter of 'signing the contract according to all the clauses' or is it a matter of Christ Himself?"

A brand new kind of life

"Since you became alive again, so to speak, when Christ arose from the dead, now set your sights on the rich treasures and joys of heaven where He sits beside God in the place of honor and power. Let heaven fill your thoughts; don't spend your time worrying about things down here. You should have as little desire for this world as a dead person does. Your real life is in heaven with Christ and God. And when Christ who is our real life comes back again, you will shine with Him and share in all His glories.

"Away then with sinful, earthly things; deaden the evil desires lurking within you; have nothing to do with sexual sin, impurity, lust and shameful desires; don't worship the good things of this life, for that is idolatry. God's terrible anger is upon those who do such things. You used to do them when your life was still part of this world; but now is the time to cast off and throw away all these rotten garments of anger, hatred, cursing and dirty language.

"Don't tell lies to each other; it was your old life with all its wickedness that did that sort of thing; now it is dead and gone. You are living a brand new kind of life that is continually learning more and more of what is right, and trying constantly to be more and more like Christ who created this new life within you.

"In this new life one's nationality or race or education or social position is unimportant; such things mean nothing. Whether a person has Christ is what matters, and He is equally available to all. Since you have been chosen by God who has given you this new kind of life, and because of His deep love and concern for you, you should practice tenderhearted mercy and kindness to others. Don't worry about making a good impression on them but be ready to suffer quietly and patiently. Be gentle and ready to forgive; never hold grudges. Remember, the Lord forgave you, so you must forgive others.

"Most of all, let love guide your life for then the whole church will stay together in perfect harmony. Let the peace of heart which comes from Christ be always present in your hearts and lives, for this is your responsibility and privilege as members of His body. And always be thankful.

"Remember what Christ taught and let His words enrich your lives and make you wise; teach them to each other and sing them out in psalms and hymns and spiritual songs, singing to the Lord with thankful hearts. And whatever you do or say, let it be as a representative of the Lord Jesus, and come with Him into the presence of God the Father to give Him your thanks" (Col. 3:1–17—*Living New Testament, Paraphrased*).

Performance or experience?

The first nine verses of this passage sound like something right out of the "Christian rulebook." It sounds like Paul is pouring it on with the old do's and don'ts. It sounds like Religion with a capital "R"—until you come to verse ten. Whether you became a Christian last night, last year or fifteen years ago, "You are living a brand new kind of life that is continually learning more and more of what is right, and trying constantly to be more and more like Christ who created this new life within you" (v. 10). There's the difference. Again and again, in all of his letters in the New Testament, Paul pounds home the idea that being a Christian means being invaded by a new life, a new power—by Christ Himself. This was the kind of power that got Christianity off the ground and kept it from being shot down when all the odds were completely against its survival.

In his preface to *Letters to Young Churches,* J. B. Phillips describes the early Christians and their faith in Christ. "The great difference between present-day Christianity and that of which we read in these letters is that to us [Christianity] is primarily a performance, to them it was a real experience. We are apt to reduce the Christian religion to a code, or at best a rule of heart and life. To these men it is quite plainly the invasion of their lives by a new quality of life altogether. They do not hesitate to describe this as Christ "living in" them. . . . These early Christians were on fire with the conviction that they had become, through Christ, literally sons of God."*

As John Rydgren, radio personality who communicates Jesus Christ over rock music stations, has put it: "Christ fits everywhere in life . . . and they say that when He fits He makes a difference in what you do . . . how you do it . . . where you do it . . . and why. They say He doesn't squeeze life out of you . . . He pumps it into you, you know, like straight from God. They say He opens the lid on life."**

This whole thing about Christianity being real

*Letters to Young Churches, J. B. Phillips, Macmillan, copyright 1947, see p. xiv.
**Silhouette Segments, John Rydgren. American Lutheran Church, Dept. of TV/Films/Radio, copyright 1966.

and seeing more change in your life hinges on one basic decision that you have to make. Just who is the real boss in your life?

One young kid—a fellow in trouble with the law off the streets of the inner city, puts it this way: "Who's the boss? You know who the boss is in the life of a junkie—or a wino? It's dope and booze. But everybody's got a boss—of some kind. Like never being able to make up your mind, or being scared of what friends will think, or even just not caring. Lots of other things we could list, so who's your boss?"

And so the Christian has to decide, "Who is my boss?" Vonda Kay Van Dyke, Miss America of 1965 makes it plain that the Christian who wants to see changes in his life for the better has got to get it straight about just who he is "working for." "When you give your whole life to God," writes Vonda, "He begins to tell you what to do. You're not the boss any more, and that's a great relief! You will be shocked when you look back and realize how clumsily you were trying to run your life.

"Maybe you don't like the thought of letting someone else make your decisions. Well, I wouldn't like it either, if it had to be another human being. We're all imperfect, but at least I'm on familiar terms with my own faults—I wouldn't want my life to depend on someone else's poor judgment. But God isn't just another person. He is love itself and He is absolutely perfect. His judgment is flawless and He'll never let you down."*

*That Girl in Your Mirror, Vonda Kay Van Dyke. Fleming H. Revell, copyright 1966, pp. 84,85.

In his book *Are You for Real?* author Larry Richards quotes a sixteen year-old from Ontario, Canada who says, "Whenever I fail in the Christian life . . . I've always been told it was because I was trying to live in my own strength. They tell me to let go [of my pride]—very easily said, but, to me as well as my friends, very hard to accomplish. Please tell us *how* we are to [have] God live His life through us and have less . . . self-effort so we can succeed in the Christian life."*

Yes, how do you go about "letting go and letting God"? In the following open-end story you will see how two young men have reacted toward Christianity. One claims he "tried religion" and it didn't work. The other teeters on the fence. Perhaps you will identify with one of these people—or perhaps you have an answer that you could give to Craig as he tries to decide . . .

Is It Real or Phony?

Craig, a senior in high school, has an older friend, Tim, who is in his second year at State College. Although Tim is three years older, Craig considers him a real friend. The boys grew up just a few houses from each other and have always shared mutual interests. In the summer when Tim is home from school, he and Craig spend hours together working on their cars. They also share an interest in Tim's field at college—science.

Recently Craig wrote to Tim, telling him that he had mailed his application to State—the college

Are You for Real?, Larry Richards, p. 144.

Tim attends. Now Craig has an answer back from Tim. Here's the letter . . .

Hi Craig:

Great to know that maybe you'll be coming up here to school next year. You'll really like the life here. The way I read you last summer, your folks really bug you. Here at school you'll be on your own—none of the pressures a fellow gets at home. The school is so big that nobody interferes with you doing your own thing.

The girls here are something else again. Most of them go along with *anything*.

What's happening on the home front? Are you still dating Marge? Last summer I remember our discussion about her crowd trying pills and pot. I didn't think much of the idea then, but I think I "get their message" now. Girls are only one interesting experiment up here. You can also get anything you want in the line of drugs, including LSD.

You may be wondering about what happened to my church kick and me feeding you that jazz about "being a changed person" and all that. I can't figure out how I ever got so high on religion, because as far as I'm concerned now, it's just not real.

You see, Craig, I tried to reform, but nothing ever happened. There wasn't any real change. I prayed . . . nothing. I went to church for over six months . . . nothing—absolutely zero.

I tried reading the Bible—even made a good crack at "reading the Bible through"—but man, it was strictly as dry as dust.

I'm not sure if God is dead, but as far as I'm concerned, the church passed away a long time ago. There is just too much hypocrisy. None of the religious guys here at school ever get involved in what's going on. There's just one word to describe the church and as far as I'm concerned that word is "phony." I've had my fill of people who claim to live Christian lives and don't. I've had my fill of trying to do it myself and just not making it.

Look, I've got to catch a class. Let me know when you get your letter of acceptance from State.

Peace . . . sincerely . . . yours truly and all that kind of stuff.

Tim

That's the letter, but what Tim doesn't know is that just a couple of months ago Craig accepted Christ at a youth rally. Craig's even been meeting with a group of fellows once a week for Bible study. But, just reading Tim's letter has started all kinds of questions. Craig is really shook. He wonders—"Is Tim right? Is this the way I'll feel in a few months? Is Christianity phony or could it be that Tim never really understood what Christianity was all about? What about the changes I thought Christianity would make in my life? Tim says he tried and couldn't change . . . can I?"

What should Craig do?

One of Tim's reasons for "chucking religion" was because he didn't see that it made any difference in his life. Do you think Tim gave up too soon and just didn't give himself "enough time to reform"?

Tim describes the church as "dead" and Christians as "phony." Does he have a point?

According to Tim, he tried to read the Bible and found it "dry." Is it important to read the Bible? What part does the Bible play in the Christian's life?

In Tim's letter he says that he prayed but nothing happened. How necessary is prayer in the Christian's life? Why should Christians pray?

If you could talk with Craig, what would you say to convince him of the realness of Christianity? What phrases from Col. 3:1–17 (see pp. 37,38) could you use to help Tim understand the difference between "trying religion" and trusting Jesus Christ?

WHAT CAN YOU DO?

The following are two columns—one with negative remarks and the other with positive statements. Between the two columns is a scale from 1–7. Rate yourself on this scale according to the way you believe you are leaning in regard to each pair of statements. For example, the first pair of statements is "I worry a lot," (negative) and "I seldom worry, I just say that's God's problem." Would you say that you lean in the direction of the negative or the positive statement? How far do you lean? For example, you might think that you are somewhere near the middle of the scale but if anything, you lean a little bit toward the negative remark, so you might get a "3." On the other hand, you might think that you lean quite a bit toward the positive remark, so you might check a "6." Or, you might think you are sort of "half and half" worrying a lot on certain occasions and not worrying so much on others, so you might check "4"—in other words, you are right in the middle. All of these statements are based on Col. 3:1–17. When you get all through checking the scale, see how your "Personal Attitude" score matches up with Col. 3:10: "You are living a brand new kind of life that is continually learning more and more of what is right, and trying constantly to be more and more like Christ who created this new life within you."

PERSONAL ATTITUDE TEST

Negative	1	2	3	4	5	6	7	Positive
"I worry a lot."	__	__	__	__	__	__	__	"I seldom worry, I just say that's God's problem."
"Sex bothers me. The way people talk, there must be something dirty about it."	__	__	__	__	__	__	__	"I understand my sexuality and I accept it."
"I have problems controlling my sexual feelings. When I see (name of someone you know) I think about going to bed together."	__	__	__	__	__	__	__	"I'm aware of sexual feelings and desires, but feel that they are under control."

Negative	1	2	3	4	5	6	7	Positive
"Let's face it, money, a car, clothes . . . these are very important to me. I've **got** to have them."								"Money talks, but it doesn't have the last word in my life. God does."
"I have a lot of deep feelings against certain groups or races. I suppose you could call it hate."								"I'm not really mad at anybody and I believe that a Christian should accept everyone just as God has accepted him."
"I don't mean to cuss, but every now and then the words slip out. I can't help it."								"Cursing isn't one of my hang-ups. To use God's name in vain is no temptation for me."
"Let's face it, I get a kick out of dirty jokes and remarks with double meanings. They're good for laughs."								"Shady stories and shady talk hold no appeal. It all seems kind of sick as far as I'm concerned."
"Sure I lie a lot. Doesn't everybody?"								"Telling the truth isn't always easy, but it does pay off in the end."
"You've got to be able to dish it out and to take it too. Nobody is going to look out for you but yourself."								"The Golden Rule makes a lot of sense to me, and I pray daily for strength to obey it."
"When somebody does me dirt, I never forget it. Once you're on my blacklist you are through."								"Forgiving isn't always easy but I feel better when I do. Holding grudges just doesn't go along with following Christ."
"There isn't much purpose in life today. The whole world is on a trip and it's one big bummer."								"Thank God for Jesus Christ and what He's done for me and the whole world. I don't understand it all, but it's something to hold onto. Christ gives me hope."

Keep in mind that Col. 3:10 doesn't mean that you have to "do what is right under your own power." The idea is to turn yourself over to Christ. Make Him your model. Follow Him. As John 15:7 puts it, "Abide with Him" . . . that is, live with Him, have Him in your daily life and in all that you do. Then the positive side of this chart will become more and more of a reality for you as you find out who you really are.

If some of the "negatives" in the "Personal Attitude Test" really bother you, see if you can talk to someone about it—another friend perhaps, or a youth director, pastor, etc. Put the date on which you took this "Personal Attitude Test" somewhere on this page and take the test again in three to six months. See if you can find any improvement in certain areas. Keep in mind that Col. 3:10 is the key to improvement.

"... the important thing ... is ... stirring up goodness and peace and joy from the Holy Spirit" Romans 14:17

WHY CAN'T
I DO
MY OWN THING?

"Doing your own thing" is definitely "in" these days. "Born Free" is everyone's theme song as we all try to follow our hearts.

The trouble is, our hearts aren't infallible guides. Further, what we want to do doesn't always match up with accepted standards of right and wrong (for example, the speed limits).

And, when we come to the standards laid down

by Christians, things get stickier than ever. The "freedom trail" talked about in the Bible seems to get muddied up with religious "do's and dont's." All too often, we wind up "stuck in the circumstances" because of the freedom that we supposedly have in Christ. We get criticized by family, friends, and society in general because we don't conform to what they think "a good Christian" is and does.

This business of being "all bogged down in our Christian freedom" and being judged by others because of our actions is not exactly a problem that is limited to the space age. Differences between "what is right," and "what is wrong," and "how free a person can really be," have existed long before the days of the "new morality." Start talking about "right and wrong," and you are bound to get an "interesting discussion" underway. (See "Peanuts" cartoon.)

The first Christian believers had their own hassle about right and wrong and how free a person is to do "his own thing." Their particular hang-ups were not always like ours, but the principles were the same. Paul talks about these principles in a letter he wrote to the Christian believers in Rome. If you know anything about first century Rome, you know that they didn't exactly roll up the sidewalks at 7 o'clock on Saturday night.

Rome was a dangerous place to turn anybody loose with the idea that "I'm completely free." The pagan society that surrounded the Roman Christians threatened to corrupt them. Their battle about "Should we or should we not eat meat offered to idols?" was no small matter. And because a pagan

48

49

society surrounds Christians today and also threatens to corrupt *them,* the principles that we find in the "meat offered to idols" controversy are still useful . . .

Freedom has a price tag

"So don't criticize each other any more. Try instead to live in such a way that you will never make your brother stumble by letting him see you doing something he thinks is wrong. As for myself, I am perfectly sure on the authority of the Lord Jesus that there is nothing really wrong with eating meat that has been offered to idols. But if someone believes it is wrong, then he shouldn't do it because for him it is wrong. And if your brother is bothered by what you eat, you are not acting in love if you go ahead and eat it. Don't let your eating ruin someone for whom Christ died.

"Don't do anything that will cause criticism against yourself even though you know that what you do is right. For, after all, the important thing for us as Christians is not what we eat or drink but stirring up goodness and peace and joy from the Holy Spirit. If you let Christ be Lord in these affairs, God will be glad; and so will your friends. In this way aim for harmony in the church and try to build each other up.

"Don't undo the work of God for a chunk of meat. Remember, there is nothing wrong with the meat, but it is wrong to eat it if it makes another stumble. The right thing to do is to quit eating meat or drinking wine or doing anything else that offends your brother or makes him sin. You may know that there is nothing wrong with what you do, even from God's point of view, but keep it to yourself; don't flaunt your faith in front of others who might be hurt by it. In this situation, happy is the man who does not sin by doing what he knows is

50

right. But anyone who believes that something he wants to do is wrong shouldn't do it. He sins if he does, for he thinks it is wrong, and so for him it *is* wrong. Anything that is done apart from what he feels is right is sin" (Rom. 14:13–23—*Living New Testament, Paraphrased*).

Christians are "born again free" if . . .

At first glance, this passage seems to concentrate on some sort of local hassle that was going on concerning menu planning in Roman households. But there is a lot more being said here than that. What Paul is laying down here is the foundation for any kind of society—Christian and otherwise. Paul talks about freedom, but he also talks about responsibility.

As some philosopher has said, "We are most free when we discover that we are not free." Double talk? No, what this man is saying is that all freedom has to exist and operate within certain boundaries—the boundaries or fences that are erected because of a person's responsibility to use his freedom correctly.

To expect the privileges of freedom without accepting its responsibilities is to ignore reality. In other words, it's just a case of "schizophrenic ethics."

As this planet becomes more and more overcrowded, freedom for all of us becomes more and more limited, simply because we have to live together. For example, somebody might feel "very free" about staying up till all hours road testing his new Honda 350 on some residential street. But, this freedom is not exactly compatible with the freedom of said Honda jockey's neighbors to get a good night's sleep.

To put it simply, "The freedom for each one of us ends where the nose of somebody else begins."

Now, you can ignore this "fact of life." You can say, "I don't care where somebody else's nose begins. If it gets in my way, I'll just rearrange it a little or run right over it." Yes, you can do that. Lots of people are trying it and many more have tried it down through the centuries. The result has been war, anarchy, chaos, rioting, etc., "ad homicidum."

Now Paul knew that this concept of "I'm going to do my own thing and nuts to everybody else" was not only impractical; it wasn't exactly what one would call loving, Christian and spiritual.

Paul also knew that there are many areas of life where one can be "irresponsibly free" but it's not exactly a life or death matter. Every society has its taboos, its rules, its regulations and its legalists who try to push their brand of "morality" on everybody else. When you get down to the "nitty gritty" of life and start deciding what is right and what is wrong and when a person is free and not free to do, things get very, very sticky and very, very hairy. You wind up with a real mess. This was the kind of problem that Paul was talking about when he discussed "eating meat" that had been offered to idols. In first century Rome, the predominant religion was dedicated to the worship of hundreds of various pagan idols and deities; topped, of course, by the "No. 1 god of the establishment"—Caesar, the king of the Roman Empire himself. There was a great deal of sacrificing of various kinds of animals to these various kind of idols and prime animals were used for the purpose.

Not being wasteful, the Romans would then take the butchered beef, or whatever, down to the local market place and sell the carcass to one of the butcher shops, at a cut rate. The butchers, in turn, would peddle the meat to the public; and in the "public" of course, were many Christians who felt no hesitation about buying this kind of meat and taking it home for the family stew pot. These Christians realized that they were free in Christ and that pagan idols represented nothing that was real and nothing that really mattered in their lives. The meat was perfectly good, clean and pure, and that was all that mattered to them. There were, however, other Christian believers, who looked back on their days of pagan superstition with many bitter memories and much disgust. To them, it seems that this kind of meat was "contaminated" because of the original purpose it had served. It was as if some sort of "evil spirit" hovered over the meat and ruined it for these Christians. It could be stamped "Grade A" as far as health standards were concerned, but spiritually, the stuff was as deadly as a pot of ptomaine stew.

Now it so happened that one Christian who felt that the meat was perfectly all right would invite another Christian over who abhorred the idea of eating "meat offered to idols." Naturally, in casual conversation the host might mention where he got the meat and his guest might promptly excuse himself to relieve the green look on his face. The whole problem was becoming more and more serious and Paul decided to write about it for two reasons: (1)

he wanted to help the Roman Christians settle a sticky little issue that was not helping them get about the real business at hand, which was bringing the Gospel to a pagan society; (2) he wanted to lay down principles that anyone could use any time, in any place, and in any century for deciding how he would balance his personal freedom with his personal responsibility to God and to others.

So, Paul simply says that he realizes that there is nothing wrong with eating meat that was offered to idols (v. 14) but Paul also realizes that he has a responsibility to all Christians (not just to those who enjoy a good steak, just as he does, and don't care where it came from). And that's why he goes on to say that if your Christian brother is bugged by the source of your filet mignons, then you are not really loving that brother if you go ahead and eat them and tell him that he is too straightlaced. "Don't let your eating ruin someone for whom Christ died," is the way Paul puts it in v. 15. The idea is that this "weaker brother" might see you eating this meat offered to idols, decide that idols really aren't so bad after all, and go right back to the pagan worship that he had left behind when he had come to Christ.

The analogies to modern day "taboos" are easily seen. Tobacco, alcohol, movies, cosmetics, dancing, television, clothing styles, even mixed bathing on the beach—all these and many others are still sharply (and unfortunately even bitterly) disputed among Christians. What is "spiritual" in one group or church can be anathema or heresy in another. As the old saying has it, "one man's poison is another man's meat," and this could have easily originated out of this controversy concerning meat offered to idols.

And so, how does the Christian "call his shots"? Is he to run around in a continual state of complete fear and frustration because his next move might cause someone to go to hell? Is the Christian to be intimidated by "his weaker brothers" (many of whom make something of a career of being very spiritual and second-guessing everyone else on what is right and what is wrong)? This kind of life would be anything but free and it doesn't sound any too responsible, either. But what Paul *is* saying here is that when it comes to handling your personal freedom, you need to have your values straight and your motives straight. Your values should center in God and Jesus Christ. As Paul says in Rom. 14:12, each of us will give an account of himself to God. So, no matter what the question, you can ask yourself, "Am I doing this because I have thought it through and evaluated it in light of my love for Christ and my total Christian experience, or am I doing this because social, cultural and religious pressure tells me that it is right (or wrong as the case may be)?"

Or, to reverse the question, "Am I doing this because Christ is my Lord?" or just because "I want to do my own thing and I don't really want anybody else interfering with my pleasure?"

Bring this down to a real life problem and you immediately begin to see where the sticky part comes in. For example, there is this question of "What is right and wrong for Sunday activities?"

55

True, there seems to be less and less controversy over this. But there still are disagreements about what is proper and improper when it comes to upholding the commandment to keep the Sabbath Day holy (and let's not cop out by saying that the Sabbath was Saturday and Christians worship on Sunday—the principle is the same).

Take this matter of being a professional athlete who has to play on Sunday. This isn't an easy decision for professional Christian athletes to make. And, there is a difference in opinion among them. Donn Moomaw, three time all-American with UCLA in the early 1950's, turned down a lucrative contract for professional football in America because he would have to play on Sunday. He went to the Canadian league instead (they play on Saturday) and had several successful seasons there before going into the ministry. Bill Glass, on the other hand, has been an all-pro with the Cleveland Browns and he has this to say in his book *My Greatest Challenge:*

"I've chosen pro football as a profession for these years of my life because I believe that I can become what God intended me to be more fully in pro football than anywhere else. I believe that He wants me to share my faith with people everywhere . . . I know pro football has given me entry into the lives of thousands of people, young and old alike. I thank God for the opportunity to use pro football to His glory and be involved in a great cause in the world."*

*My Greatest Challenge, Bill Glass. Copyright 1968, Word Books, p. 181.

In his book *Get in the Game* Glass says: "I believe that Christian athletes have an opportunity to do a great deal of good by playing Sunday football . . . I made my decision to play pro football on the basis of the great platform that it gave me from which to influence people. People are interested in what the pro has to say. They may not listen to the pastor, but they would listen to a pro football player. I just couldn't believe that God was willing for all pro sports to go without a witness just because of Sunday game days."*

Who's right? Moomaw or Glass? You might argue that one with someone for a long time, but the point that you should see here is that both of these men evaluated their Christian freedom according to their own convictions and personal relationship to Jesus Christ. They thought through how they could best be used by God and they used their freedom in Christ accordingly.

"But wouldn't Glass cause some Christians to stumble?" you might ask. Well, let's be honest. That's quite possible. But any weaker brother (if he wanted to be fair) would have to examine Glass's entire position and his clearly stated motives for playing pro football. Any "weaker brother" couldn't just waggle his finger and say "Because you play pro football on Sunday, I may go back to my pagan ways and be lost forever to the Christian cause." Glass is playing pro football on Sunday because he believes that it is the way to reach people for Jesus

Get in the Game, Bill Glass, Copyright 1965, Word Books, pp. 117, 118.

57

Christ. That's a lot different from playing pro football on Sunday because he likes to make a quick buck and could care less about what anybody thinks about how he handles his Christian freedom.

Admittedly, it isn't easy to think through the sticky problems and come up crystal clear answers for "What is right for me? How do I handle my freedom and responsibilities?"

Perhaps one of the stickiest areas for young people, at least, is the vast field of rock music. Most adults don't like it and most teen-agers lash back by listening to all the more of it because "it's our music and what do the adults know about it anyway?" There seems to be little doubt that there is a "generation gap," when it comes to this business of musical taste. So, what are Christian young people to do about rock music? Many have already made their choice. They're going to listen to it and they don't really care what the adults say. But, that's no real answer. That is simply saying "I'm going to do my own thing and I could care less if you agree or not."

In the following "hypothetical story" the make-believe characters come up with a very real problem. There is more to rock music than the beat. There are the lyrics, and the whole concept of what some songs are trying to do. Read it and see if you hear any echoes from Roman butcher shops in the background . . .

Rock-a My Soul Or ???

Steve has a lot going for him. He's on the varsity track team, he's president of the youth group at church, and he's dating Margie, the class beauty queen, on a "steadily" basis.

Most important for Steve, however, is "The Sounds"—the "Gospel-Rock" group that he and three other fellows from the church started last year. Recently, the group was the featured musical ensemble at the district youth rally and they went over big.

The four boys in "The Sounds" work several hours each week on lyrics and arrangements. The lyrics show that Steve and the other fellows have a good understanding of Christianity and that they are really trying to communicate their faith with the words and sounds they put together.

"Sound" is the big thing, and the fellows are always listening to a record or have a radio going full blast. "It's research," is Steve's explanation to his mother and dad, or anybody else who asks. "We've got to discover the ways the various rock groups use sounds and the beat. That's how we get new ideas."

But late last Friday afternoon something came up that caused Steve to do some heavy thinking all through the weekend. He and the other three fellows in "The Sounds" were sprawled in front of the stereo at Steve's house listening to a new record by "The Doors." Came a knock at the door, and there was the church youth director—Jim Franklin.

"Oh, hi Jim," said Steve. "Come on in. We're just grooving with a new record I just brought home."

"Can't stay long, man," said Jim. "But I did want to talk a minute about next Sunday night's youth meeting and what you guys are going to do for your part of the program."

So Jim came in and sat down while "The Doors" finished doing their thing. As the record concluded, Jim observed, "That sounds great, I'll have to admit it, but the lyrics are sure sick."

"What do you mean the lyrics are sick?" asked Bob, one of the members of the group. "I very seldom listen to the lyrics, anyway."

"Yea," Steve chimed in. "We don't dig some of the stuff that 'The Doors' have done, but we do like to do research on a good sound. That's one of the reasons why we go over so well with the kids."

"OK, OK," laughed Jim. "I'm not putting the pinch on you guys for playing immoral music. I'm just saying that a lot of this rock music stuff can suck you into listening to a lot of garbage because you like the sound. According to the lyrics in that song, the only thing worth doing is having sex—premarital, extramarital, or any other kind—and all that that amounts to is something to pass your time. The thing is absolute dirt and completely contrary to the teachings in the Bible."

"But we don't dig the lyrics, Jim," replied Steve with some concern. "We really don't. The music is what we're after and we believe that this is a way to really reach kids today with Christ's message. Are you telling us to cool it on listening to rock music records?"

"I'm not telling you guys to do anything," said Jim. "That's really not in my job description. I'm supposed to help you get better acquainted with Jesus Christ and the freedom He gives everyone who wants to follow Him. But there is this idea in the Bible about balancing your freedom with your sense of responsibility and you are responsible to God for how you program your computer—that little pea up there called your brain."

"What do you mean by 'program your computer'?" asked Dick, the bass guitar player for the group. "What does brain power have to do with listening to a good beat?"

"There is more to it than just the beat, Dick," Jim replied. "In the computer trade they've got a saying called GIGO, which means 'garbage in, garbage out.' In other words, whatever you feed into the machine is what it's going to spit back at you. And when you listen to some of these sick songs by 'The Doors' and other groups of questionable origin, you can't help but be affected by the whole ball of wax —the beat and the lyrics, and the total impact of what they're trying to do on the record."

"But it's like Steve says, Jim, we don't listen to the lyrics" chimed in Bob, the group's drummer.

"Don't you? There have been studies made that show that kids do hear the lyrics and do eventually memorize them. Think about it for yourself. You know the lyrics to that song you just played by 'The Doors' because you knew what I was talking about when I chopped it down for being sick on sex."

"So what do you want us to do?" asked Steve. "Are we supposed to trade in our guitars, drums and amplifiers for an organ and a year's supply of Bach sonatas?"

"No, I'm not telling you to trade in anything. I'm just telling you that you have the freedom to do your thing with rock music for the glory of God, but you also have the responsibility to use it right. Just think about it. Does your research have to include 'The Doors' and some of these other groups dedicated to grubbifying America? Don't forget that you guys are looked up to by the rest of the kids at church and by plenty of kids outside our church. When they hear you talking about 'The Doors' and some of these other groups and making no qualifications about what is good and what is rotten, what's their conclusion? It must be OK to listen to any of this stuff. Steve and the other guys do and they're such neat Gospel-rock singers."

"Back off, man," Steve laughed. "You're getting a little close and I think I'd better talk this one over with my henchmen. Why don't I call you back after dinner and we'll go over what we're going to do for Sunday night."

And so, as Jim drove away, Steve turned to the other fellows. He could see that Bob was really uptight and not at all happy with what Jim had said. Dick had a puzzled look on his face and Tom was about to put on another record. What could Steve say? Was Jim right? How did one keep the ledgers even in this business of freedom and responsibility?

What should Steve (and the others) do?

Does it sound like the youth director is completely against all rock music? What is the youth director actually trying to tell Steve and the others?

Do you think that the youth director is right? Do teen-agers eventually memorize the lyrics to rock songs—dirty words and all? What about all the double and triple meanings in a lot of the rock music numbers that are coming out weekly? What about the open boasting of people such as Frank Zappa, leader of the "Mothers of Invention," who has said: "The loud sounds and bright lights of today are tremendous indoctrination tools. Is it possible to modify the human chemical structure with the right combination of frequencies? . . . If the right kind of beat makes you tap your foot, what kind of beat makes you curl your fist and strike?"*

If you apply Paul's teaching in Romans 14 to this situation, what is the "chunk of meat" being discussed? (See Rom. 14:20.) What about Rom. 14:17? "For, after all, the important thing for us as Christians is not what we eat or drink (or listen to) but stirring up goodness and peace and joy from the Holy Spirit" (Living New Testament). Can "The Sounds" continue their Gospel-rock work and stir up goodness, peace and joy from the Holy Spirit? How?

In Rom. 14:21, Paul clearly says, "The right thing to do is to quit eating meat or drinking wine or doing anything else that offends your brother or makes him sin." Suppose some of the adults in the church come to "The Sounds" and tell them that their music is offensive. Should they quit playing in the church? (Would moving to another church and playing elsewhere really solve the problem?) What if, by chance, some fellow teen-agers criticized the Gospel-rock approach? What could the boys say? What did Paul mean when he said "offends your brother or makes him sin?"

*From "That Music," the American Observer.

WHAT CAN YOU DO?

Take the following "Freedom/Responsibility" quiz to see just how free you really feel in some areas that are important in your life.

FREEDOM/RESPONSIBILITY QUIZ

AREA OF INTEREST OR CONCERN	FEEL STIFLED HERE?	FEEL GOOD BALANCE HERE?	WANT OR HAVE TOO MUCH FREEDOM HERE?
Rock Music	———	———	———
Radio	———	———	———
TV	———	———	———
Movies	———	———	———
Dancing	———	———	———
Dating	———	———	———
Curfew Times	———	———	———
Studies-schoolwork	———	———	———
Money	———	———	———
Time	———	———	———
Friends	———	———	———

This chapter sums up the first section of this book, which deals with the general topic, "Who Am I?" To get a better perspective of how the first four chapters have (or have not) influenced your attitudes and ideas, take the following quiz. Keep in mind that this quiz doesn't begin to cover all facets of the question "Who am I?" These five questions, however, can help you think about key attitudes as far as your Christian life is concerned.

AGREE OR DISAGREE

STATEMENT	AGREE	DISAGREE	NOT SURE YET
1. I know I can love others because I know that I am loved by God.	___	___	___
2. I believe that with the help of the Holy Spirit I have the opportunity to become my real Christian self because I have a choice between righteousness and sin.	___	___	___
3. I know that God's idea of my real self is far better and finer than any ideas I have and I want His plan for my life.	___	___	___
4. I know that as I relate more completely to and identify with Jesus Christ, I can become all that God has in mind for me to be.*	___	___	___
5. Freedom to "do my own thing" must be balanced against my responsibility to God and to others.	___	___	___

*See Romans 5:2, *Living New Testament, Paraphrased.*

CHAPTER 6

"If you love someone you will be loyal to him no matter what the cost" I Corinthians 13:7

LOVE MY ENEMIES? WHAT ABOUT MY FRIENDS?

"Love my enemies! I have a hard enough time with my friends!"

Ever mutter something like that? Ever at least think something like that after the preacher (or preachy type) admonishes you to smile through your bloody teeth, turn the other cheek and be nice to those who clobber you physically or mentally? We often feel like saying, "Pastor, one thing at a time. I can't seem to get along too well with my friends, let alone love my enemies. I'd like a few tips on 'winning friends and keeping them.' *Then* I might go on to graduate school and try this 'love your enemies bit'."

Let's face it, loving anybody is hard, whether he's a friend or an enemy. What can a Christian do, where can he start and how does he start? Honorable Chinese philosopher has said, "journey of a thousand miles begins with first step." So to have friends, be one (see Prov. 18:24). But how do you go about that? Well, it's spelled out in one of the most quoted chapters in the entire Bible—I Corinthians 13.

One of the troubles with I Corinthians 13, however, is that it is in King James English (in an awful lot of Bibles, at least). It sounds so "beautiful" it doesn't seem real. But the Bible wasn't originally written in Elizabethan prose. It was written in Koine Greek—the language of the man on the street. So, put I Corinthians 13 in 20th century "man on the street" terms, and it starts to make more sense. It starts to look like you can get a clue on how to take that first step toward loving friends and being kind to enemies.

What is this thing called love?

"If I had the gift of being able to speak in other languages without learning them, and could speak in every language there is in all of heaven and earth, but didn't love others, I would only be making noise. If I had the gift of prophecy and knew all about what is going to happen in the future, knew everything about *everything*, but didn't love others, what good would it do? Even if I had the gift of faith so that I could speak to a mountain and make it move, I would still be worth nothing at all without love. If I gave everything I have to poor people, and if I were burned alive for preaching the Gospel but didn't love others, it would be of no value whatever.

"Love is very patient and kind, never jealous or envious, never boastful or proud, never haughty or selfish or rude. Love does not demand its own way. It is not irritable or touchy. It does not hold grudges and will hardly even notice when others do it wrong. It is never glad about injustice, but rejoices whenever truth wins out. If

67

you love someone you will be loyal to him no matter what the cost. You will always believe in him, always expect the best of him, and always stand your ground in defending him.

"All the special gifts and powers from God will some day come to an end, but love goes on forever. Some day prophecy, and speaking in unknown languages, and special knowledge—these gifts will disappear. Now we know so little, even with our special gifts, and the preaching of those most gifted is still so poor. But when we have been made perfect and complete, then the need for these inadequate special gifts will come to an end, and they will disappear.

"It's like this: when I was a child I spoke and thought and reasoned as a child does. But when I became a man my thoughts grew far beyond those of my childhood, and now I have put away the childish things. In the same way, we can see and understand only a little about God now, as if we were peering at His reflection in a poor mirror; but some day we are going to see Him in His completeness, face to face. Now all that I know is hazy and blurred, but then I will see everything clearly, just as clearly as God sees into my heart right now.

"There are three things that remain—faith, hope and love—and the greatest of these is love" (I Corinthians 13—*Living New Testament, Paraphrased*).

Good grief! Must I become a saint?

It almost seems as if sainthood is being asked for in a passage like I Corinthians 13. Not only are you to be a good guy on a white horse; you are supposed to give away the horse and walk through the desert yourself. It helps, however, if you slice I Corinthians 13 about three ways: vs. 1–4 tell you to be real; vs. 5–7 tell you to put others first; and vs. 8–13 tell you to "be in touch"—that is, with God.

A lot of us face real hang-ups when it comes to this business of "being real." In fact, from the cradle on, most people are taught to "communicate on a phony level." They are taught to wear certain masks at certain times. You never tell your hostess the dinner was lousy (even though you are gasping with ptomaine). You tell her it was wonderful, delicious. This is what is known as being "polite." You never admit that you have a splitting headache and want to go home. You stick it out and try to be the smiling life of the party. A basic rule for social acceptance is "be kind, considerate . . . don't hurt anyone's feelings." Now, all this is fine and it is true that we should not go around slashing at everyone's ego with gay abandon. On the other hand, a lot of what passes for politeness and courtesy is really a phony cover-up for feelings that range from disdain to hatred.

With some people, however, the problem is that they "enjoy" being phony and maybe just a little bit sneaky. They don't trust anyone else and they don't really expect anyone to trust them, and so they are constantly trying to see who they can outtalk, outmaneuver, outwit, etc. They think it is a feather in their hats when they get someone to trust them and then turn around and slip a knife into their ribs.

This is well-illustrated in the "Peanuts" cartoon on next page. Every year Charles Schulz, creator of "Peanuts," runs at least one cartoon, if not a series, on the classic theme of Lucy promising to hold the football for Charlie Brown, and Charlie Brown

holding back, telling her that he *knows* she's going to pull the ball away and Lucy finally convincing him that she is changed, that she is different, that *this* time she will hold the ball and let him kick it instead of thrashing madly at nothing but air and landing on his head.

And so, Charlie backs up, makes a run toward the ball, and naturally Lucy pulls it away. We all expect Lucy to pull it away because we all can identify quite well here. We all have had people pull the ball away from us or we have enjoyed pulling it away from them. The reason people enjoy pulling the ball away, or the reason that people are very suspicious that someone is going to pull the ball away, is that people don't really trust each other much. There isn't any real love at the base of so many relationships, and this is what Paul is basically getting at here. It isn't sweet talk, brilliance, or even "deep spirituality" that builds friendships. It's love—honestly and openly trusting one another with no hidden agendas and no false fronts.

Note, in the "Peanuts" cartoon, Charlie Brown is "sucker enough" to trust Lucy. He has "faith in human nature." Charlie symbolizes the risk that all of us need to take if real love and real friendship is to occur.

So that's the first step, and then you move on to this business of putting others ahead of yourself. One of the best ways to do this is to practice what is called empathy—putting yourself in the other guy's shoes. This "empathy" is really what Jesus was talking about when He gave us the golden rule —"Treat others as you want them to treat you"

71

(*Living New Testament*). Another thing is to accept the other person—accept his faults as well as his good qualities. Accept his hang-ups along with his attributes. Real friends accept one another. Real friends have no rivalry going and they are not out to change one another into the kind of person that would be "perfect." Psychologists will tell you that the desire to change somebody to what you think is a more perfect or improved individual is basically a hostile desire. You may want God to change someone because you can see that they are unhappy the way they are, but you let God do the changing. It's your business to do the accepting.

But the big point in I Corinthians 13 is to "be in touch." What Paul is saying in these last verses of the chapter (vs. 8–13) is that Christians have only begun to fully understand God's love and God's mysteries. "We can see and understand only a little about God now, as if we were peering at His reflection in a poor mirror; but some day we are going to see Him in His completeness, face-to-face." Then we will . . . "see everything clearly, just . . . as God sees into [our] heart[s] right now." And so, the Christian's task is clear enough: If he wants the kind of power that will enable him to accept others, to understand others and to be genuine with others, he is going to have to stay in touch with that power. The more we learn about God the more we will learn about ourselves and the more friends we will have. And, the more resources we'll have to handle the sticky situations that often come up between us and our friends. It seems that you just can't avoid these minor (and sometimes major) crises. Following is an open-end story that involves a "sticky little crisis" that arises between two high school girls. The cause of the crisis is a handsome high school boy. Solution to the crisis isn't quite so simple . . .

Should Love Bear ALL Things?

Gwen could hardly wait until she got to the school gym to tell her best friend some important news. "Oh Nancy," she gasped, "you know that new kid who came to church yesterday? He showed up in my math class today! Remember how tall, cute and . . ."

"Well, I'm glad you're in a good mood. Such a boring day," Nancy said as she dumped her books in the locker and took out her sneakers.

"And he sits right beside me," Gwen sputtered out. "He's so friendly and nice."

"Why don't ya work on him?" Nancy yawned. "Maybe you can get him to ask you to the Youth Banquet next month."

Gwen thought awhile. It was so easy for Nancy to say something like that. Guys were always asking her out. She could have a date any time she wanted with any fellow, it seemed. Nancy was that kind of girl. She always knew what to say and how to play up to a guy to get what she wanted.

Gwen tried not to envy the popular and well-liked girl. She had always been proud to be her close friend. Nancy had a way of making others feel at ease around her.

"It would be so great if I could go to the Banquet this year," Gwen sighed, "but you know how shy I am around boys."

"Oh, don't sweat it, Gwen. I'll help you."

The next few days the two girls exchanged information and worked on strategy. Gwen forced herself to be friendly and joke around with Dave, the new student, as she entered the classroom. She tried to take Nancy's advice and act casual, even though her heart seemed to thump loud enough for the whole class to hear.

One afternoon a couple of weeks later when Nancy and Gwen met in the gym, Nancy entered the locker room with lowered eyes. "Got something to tell you, Gwen," she said.

"What happened, Nancy? Why so glum?"

Nancy took a bite from the side of her fingernail. "I saw him in the library and we started talking about our church. He asked about the youth activities and stuff like that, so I thought it would be a perfect time to mention the Youth Banquet. You know he hasn't been to any of the youth meetings yet. But honest, Gwen, I had no idea he would ask me."

"What did you tell him about going?" Gwen asked anxiously.

"I didn't tell him I would go. I said I'd let him know tomorrow." Nancy studied the floor. "Listen, I can turn him down if you want me to, Gwen."

"I don't know. I'll think it over and call you tonight," said Gwen slowly.

The girls split up—Nancy to go to the park and brood about goofing things up; Gwen to return home and sit staring at the phone with the crazy hope that Dave would call. As she sat waiting, Gwen's face hardened. She had wanted to date

Dave so badly, and Nancy knew it. She thought about how Nancy had probably acted flirty, clever and talkative around him, and in her usual way had finagled the date out of him.

With jealousy and hurt stinging inside, Gwen felt betrayed by her best friend. Nancy was probably sorry and was offering to turn him down. Maybe this was a chance to get back at Nancy. What should she do? Should she take Nancy up on the offer and make her stay home from the Banquet, too? Gwen knew she could make Nancy feel guilty, so guilty she might even stay home, turning him down. That would fix her, show her what it was like to be disappointed. Imagine Nancy sitting home and not going to the biggest event at church! Gwen half smiled at the thought.

What should Gwen do?

Keeping I Corinthians 13 in mind, can Gwen go ahead and "teach Nancy a lesson"? On the other hand, suppose Gwen does go ahead and ask Nancy not to accept the date from Dave. According to I Corinthians 13, how should Nancy respond?

On the other hand, if Gwen puts on the "sweet Christian girl" act, is this the best way out? What does I Cor. 13:1–4 say about putting on acts?

How should Gwen deal with her jealous feelings? Is it any solution for her to pretend that she doesn't have them? What should Christians do about jealous feelings? Feel guilty about them and try to hide them?

If you were in a position to talk with Gwen and

Nancy, what would you say to them? What is the key to helping them mend the rift that has come between them?

WHAT CAN YOU DO?

Use the following "Love Test" to see how you measure up to the Bible's idea of real love. Check the column that you feel best describes your present attitudes, actions—the way you really are as you see yourself.

LOVE TEST

CHARACTERISTIC	I NEED HELP HERE —AND BAD!	WITH (OR TO) SOME PEOPLE, YES; OTHERS, NO	JUST FAIR	COULD BE WORSE, I GUESS	NO PROBLEM FOR ME
Patience	___	___	___	___	___
Kindness	___	___	___	___	___
Jealousy	___	___	___	___	___
Boasting	___	___	___	___	___
Pride	___	___	___	___	___
Stuck-up	___	___	___	___	___
Selfishness	___	___	___	___	___
Rudeness	___	___	___	___	___
Demand own way	___	___	___	___	___
Irritable (touchy)	___	___	___	___	___
Holding grudges	___	___	___	___	___
Judgmental	___	___	___	___	___
Loyalty	___	___	___	___	___
Thinking best of others	___	___	___	___	___

Now go back over the list and see if your check list forms any kind of a pattern. Did you check a lot in the column WITH (OR TO) SOME PEOPLE, YES; OTHER PEOPLE, NO? If you did, you might start thinking about which people you are talking about and under what conditions and circumstances. Do certain people bring out in you things like jealousy, pride, selfishness, defensiveness, impatience? Do other people bring out kindness, courtesy, loyalty, etc.? Try to analyze just why certain people affect you the way they do. What does this tell you about the friendships that you are keeping? What does this tell you about really "working at love" in your relationships with others?

Reread I Corinthians 13 and substitute the word Christ for the word "love" all the way through. Since God is love and Christ is God, it follows that Christ can fit into I Corinthians 13 perfectly. Next, think very hard about just how you are going about trying to "love others." Are you really involved with Jesus Christ, or is He just a name, a doctrine, a place that you have along with all your other neatly packaged theological premises? Remember that three things remain—faith, hope and Christ, and the greatest of these is Christ. And without Christ, you can have no love.

". . . be a new and different person . . . in all you do and think." Romans 12:2

BUT WHAT WILL EVERYONE SAY?

Important, isn't it? What people think and say about us, that is. We might as well not fake it . . . we have to admit it. We all want respect, admiration, to be liked, loved, looked up to—at least not looked down upon.

But "being in" doesn't always bring instant bliss. The crowd's standards and tastes are not always the key to freedom, happiness, achievement. Being one of the herd does not always guarantee access to heavenly bliss.

And here's another thing to think about. The crowd could really care less about you—as a person, that is. You're supposed to "come along." You're supposed to wear, say, do, think and be certain things because it's the "thing to do." But all these "in things to do" aren't dreamed up with your personal benefit in mind. Many of them are actually the products of fashion, advertising, and other power structures that are mainly interested in making a quick buck.

When you're young, it seems that there is always a tension (a war?) between the fashions of the peer group and what your elders consider "nice," "sensible," or "Christian." "Don't conform to this world," drones the minister, and he often manages to make Christianity sound like a one-way ticket to weirdoville.

But is that what the minister means to communicate? Is that what the Bible teaches? There is a lot of Scripture about not getting too cozy with the world, and there is a good reason. It goes back to this idea of just who is really interested in *your* welfare. God loves you. Because He is your creator, He is definitely interested in your welfare. Does the "world" love you? Does the world (the crowd) really care about you?

What happens if you cross God? What happens if you give Him static, disobey Him, go your own way and just plain defy Him? God forgives you when you come to Him sincerely sorry for what you have done. This is what the whole Bible is all about. God loved the world so much that after it had crossed Him and given Him every possible kind of chop, and rebuff, He sent His Son to die for the world. (For details, see John 3:16.)

But what happens if you "cross" the ever lovin' crowd? You are dead. You are out, tubed—a social leper. Does the crowd want you to think for yourself? Hardly. But God does . . . He says so in a letter that was written a long time ago, but which is very, very up-to-date . . .

The taste that never quits . . .

"And so, dear brothers, I plead with you to give your bodies to God. Let them be a living sacrifice, holy—the kind He can accept. When you think of what He has done for you, is this too much to ask?

"Don't copy the behavior and customs of this world, but be a new and different person with a fresh newness in all you do and think. Then you will learn from your own experience how His ways will really satisfy you" (Rom. 12:1,2—*Living New Testament*).

How do you conform without conforming?

Romans 12:1,2 are passages that well-meaning memory verse chairmen like to assign to young Sunday school scholars. The reason for this is really unknown, but you get a clue, at least, from these phrases such as "not copying the behavior of this world." There is a lot of behavior in this world that isn't worth copying. But then, on the other hand, there is a lot of behavior that is worth copying, so how do you tell the difference?

For example, we all conform to the codes of our society to a certain extent. Our "outward form or appearance" is like a uniform that we wear so that we can feel that we fit in with everyone else. That's why we don't wear gym clothes to a banquet or eat dinner with a butcher knife. We do or don't do certain things because it is practical and makes sense.

There is, however, that line that is so easy to cross. That line lies between conforming because it is sensible and reasonable and effective or conforming because you need the approval of the crowd, no matter what the crowd's attitude is toward the church and Christ.

Think of the word "copy" as the *Living New Testament* translates it. Why does a person cheat on a test? Isn't it because he knows he hasn't got it? He wouldn't need to cheat if he knew his material. Yet it matters so much to him to succeed in appearance that he is willing to take someone else's knowledge and pretend it is his.

And what about being a Christian? Does this make it easy to "not conform to the standards of the world?" The Christian shouldn't really need to be a copycat, to be "in," to be accepted, to gain the approval of friends. A Christian who has a growing relationship with Jesus Christ has an inner strength and he doesn't need a lot of external things to build his ego.

But, let's face it, a lot of Christians do need to be in, to be accepted, to gain approval of friends. A lot of Christians? Maybe we should be honest and say too many Christians. Maybe the reason that a lot of Christians are so intent on "going steady with the world" is that they have built a wall between themselves and God. Instead of feeling as though Christ were giving them inner strength, they feel that Christianity is just something that puts on more outer pressure. Too many Christians—especially young people—mistake Christianity for some sort of "moral marathon" or something that is supposed to help them build "a muscular character."

But that's not what the Bible really teaches. In God's eyes, the strong person is the one who can continually admit that he is weak. II Cor. 12:9 says "[God's] strength is made perfect in [our] weakness." The question isn't how hard the Christian fights against the world or how well he keeps up with his list of do's and don'ts. The question is, "Is the Christian submitting to God and allowing God to remake him on His terms?"

One of the best known "items of equipment" in the "Peanuts" cartoon strip is Linus' security blanket, which he clutches in a death grip 24 hours a day. (See cartoon.) Nothing can shake it from his grasp, not even surprise attacks by Snoopy. The reason that Linus grips that blanket day in and day out, in rain, snow, sleet or hailstorm? "The struggle for security," says Linus "knows no season!" That's very true for all of us. We all want security. Ironically, instead of finding our security in God, we find it in lists of do's and don'ts. We somehow think that "obeying the rules" is the way to be a "good Christian." But instead of turning out to be solid footing for your Christian life, the rules seem to turn into quicksand. The more you struggle, the deeper into trouble you get.

If the Christian must have a "security blanket" he should make his security blanket God Himself.

Keeping a list of do's and don'ts seems to turn out to be a lot easier if you settle this business of just who is in charge—God or you. Once you decide that God is in charge, it's amazing how many do's and don'ts aren't even an issue any more. Once you understand where your real security lies, you will find that you don't need any kind of "security blanket." You can go on and grow out of that stage to a more mature and exciting relationship with God.

Notice that these verses talk of being a new and different person in all you do and think. Perhaps these verses should be read two or three times by people who say "I'm willing to go along with a change in what I do, but as for my thoughts, that's my business!" Yet, Jesus always made it clear that the desire to sin is on the same level of the act of sin itself. In other words, what you think and what you want show what you are. What do you honestly desire? That is a good test of how different you really are. Charlie Brown (see cartoon) is a perfect example of "wishing he could change" but only when the pressure is on. The minute the pressure is taken away, Charlie goes right back to his carefree approach to life. The only thing missing in this cartoon is that Charlie didn't say a quick prayer for God to deliver him from having to give a report he didn't have ready. This is precisely what a lot of Christians do when the going gets rough—all of a sudden their prayer life improves 5,000 percent. But take off the pressure, remove the danger or the problem and they go right back to their usual pattern—unchanged and not really planning to change.

I'M DOOMED! IF THAT BELL DOESN'T RING PRETTY SOON, I'M DOOMED!

I SHOULD HAVE DONE THAT REPORT, AND THEN I WOULDN'T HAVE HAD TO WORRY LIKE THIS...

OH, PLEASE DON'T CALL ON ME... PLEASE, DON'T!

WHY DOESN'T THAT STUPID BELL RING? COME ON, BELL... RING! TAKE ME OFF THE HOOK!

PLEASE DON'T CALL ON ME TODAY... WAIT UNTIL TOMORROW... PLEASE DON'T CALL ON ME .... PLEASE! PLEASE! PLEASE! PLEASE!

COME ON, YOU STUPID BELL, RING! DON'T JUST HANG THERE ON THE WALL! RING! COME ON! RING!!

OH, I'M DOOMED! SHE'S GOING TO CALL ON ME NEXT, AND I'M NOT READY, AND...

RRING!

OH, MAN, WHAT A CLOSE CALL! I THOUGHT FOR SURE SHE WAS GOING TO CALL ON ME... I THOUGHT I WAS DOOMED!

NOW, YOU CAN GO HOME AND FINISH YOUR REPORT, HUH, CHARLIE BROWN? THEN YOU WON'T HAVE TO WORRY ABOUT IT TOMORROW...

WHO CARES ABOUT TOMORROW? C'MON, LET'S PLAY BALL!

85

So, perhaps the first thing you need to do is come right out and confess to God that you rather enjoy your lukewarm state of Christianity. Admit to Him that your spiritual life is about as lively as a corpse. Confess to God honestly that you don't really seem to want to be bothered with a lot of spiritual things.

And then go one step farther. Tell God right now that you want to want Him to come into your life at a deeper level than ever before. Tell Him you want to be able to give Him permission to win you completely to Himself. This may be painful. This may be your first honest attempt to "level" with Christ. Don't worry about it. God knows all about your hang-up or your lukewarm state—whatever it might be. He'll take you just the way you are. That's what He's been doing for quite a few years with everyone. So tell God about your hang-ups. Tell God you have a hard time walking that fine line between conforming to the world because it's sensible and running after the world with your tongue hanging out because you have to have peer-group approval. God understands and He'll help you if you really want help.

God is with us in any kind of problem, any kind of situation. Take the "open-end story" that follows. What would you do if you were in Joe's place?

"Fink or Square? Take Your Choice!"

Joe clerked every Friday and Saturday evening in Mr. Langley's drugstore. Mr. Langley was a prominent member of Joe's church, and Joe knew he was completely trusted when it came to running the store. Mr. Langley expected a lot out of a high school guy like Joe, but he always thought it important to give him time off for church activities and special youth projects that came up. In fact, Joe had just asked for next Friday night off so that he could go to the combination Christian service activity and social that the youth group was having at church.

After Mr. Langley gave his consent, he left the store and Joe hurried about getting ready for the crowd he knew would soon be there.

Since Joe has been working at the store, a group of kids from school has been coming in practically every night and has ordered hamburgers, sodas, and malts. Joe didn't know them very well at first since they weren't Christian kids, and he didn't hang around with them at school.

But in the last few weeks they've been very friendly and have invited him to sit down with them when there were no customers to wait on. Since Joe had a ten minute break anyway, he had joined them one night. They had a great time kidding around, but when the ten minutes had gone by, he got right up and went back to the counter.

"Hey, what's the big rush?" they had asked.

"Break's up," Joe had said as he rose and picked up the sponge to wipe up the counter. The kids had looked at each other and given him that if-you-say-so shrug.

After that, Joe joined them quite often. He was beginning to like those kids, and he knew they respected him and accepted him for what he was. Once as Joe was fixing a round of sundaes, they had teased him. "Aw, come on and give us an extra scoop of ice cream. Old man Langley will never know the dif."

"Sure," Joe had said. "My treat." And he gave them all the extra scoop; then dug out his wallet and put the money in the cash register. He had been surprised that night to find that they respected his honesty.

One evening as Joe prepared to leave for his job at the drug store, the phone rang. It was Bill, leader of the group of non-Christian friends that had been dropping in to see Joe on his job.

"How about coming with us next Friday night? Going skiing," said Bill.

Joe gripped the phone hard. He knew that an invitation to go skiing with Bill and the rest of his friends wasn't given to just anyone. They were willing to accept him as more than the "soda jerk who worked at the drug store." But Joe hesitated. He had just asked Mr. Langley for next Friday night off, but that was to go to the Youth Night at church. How could he tell these kids he was expected to be at church? Right now he wasn't a complete dud. They knew he was different, but he couldn't carry it too far or they would give up on him and chalk him off as a square. Certainly there was nothing wrong with going skiing with them.

But Joe thought of the church kids. They would never understand. They would find out where he had been and would give him a rough time. They would tell him that he should be at church supporting the youth program.

Finally, Joe thought of Mr. Langley and what he would say. Joe could pretty well predict. If he went skiing and Mr. Langley found out, he would tell him he had given the evening off to go to church and not skiing with a bunch of worldly kids. Joe knew if he went directly to Mr. Langley and told him he had a change of plans and wanted to go skiing instead, Mr. Langley would consider that irresponsible. Joe wanted very much to be friends with this group. He wanted to show them a Christian could have a good time without being an oddball. Yet, he didn't want to get himself "into a corner" where the group was controlling and manipulating him.

Joe looked at Bill and tried to think of how he should word his reply . . .

What should Joe do?

How can Joe avoid being a stereotype "I don't do that" kind of Christian but still have a fresh approach to this situation?

Is this a clear-cut case of choosing either the church group or the secular crowd, or do other circumstances enter the picture? If other circumstances are there, describe them.

How would you help Joe avoid the "big squeeze" of gradually being absorbed by the secular group? How can Joe keep the strength that he seemed to have when he first met Bill and the others?

What is Joe's responsibility to his employer Mr. Langley? What is his responsibility to the church young people and the church program? What is his responsibility to the non-Christians with whom he has struck up this friendship?

WHAT CAN YOU DO?

On the following page is a graph that shows the results of one study comparing the adult influence and peer-group influence on the individual at certain times during his life.

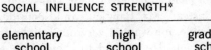

SOCIAL INFLUENCE STRENGTH*

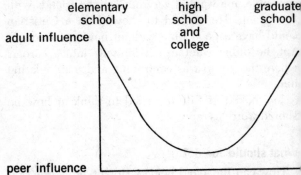

Note that through elementary school adult influence is high, but as the student gets into high school and college, adult influence plummets to practically nothing and peer-group influence takes over. As the student comes out of college and gets into graduate school or adult life adult influence again takes over (quite logically, of course, because the individual is now an adult himself). Keep in mind, however, that adults are not exactly immune to "peer-group influence." Adults have their own peer groups, too, and are very much influenced by them. This peer-group influence by adults is aptly described by the well-worn cliché "keeping up with the Joneses."

Following is a list of areas and interests in your life where your peer group may or may not have a great deal of influence over you. Examine each item carefully and then check the appropriate column at the right according to how you feel about how much the peer group really influences you in this particular area.

*Are You for Real?, Larry Richards. Copyright 1968, M.B.I., Moody Press. See p. 92.

HOW MUCH INFLUENCE?

AREA OF POSSIBLE PEER-GROUP INFLUENCE . . .	A GREAT DEAL	QUITE A BIT	SOME I SUPPOSE	HARDLY AT ALL
Clothes	_____	_____	_____	_____
Personal Grooming	_____	_____	_____	_____
What I watch on TV	_____	_____	_____	_____
What films I see	_____	_____	_____	_____
What records I buy	_____	_____	_____	_____
What I listen to on the radio	_____	_____	_____	_____
What I think about the "race problem"	_____	_____	_____	_____
What I think about the international situation—the cold war that is usually hot somewhere in the world	_____	_____	_____	_____
What I think of adults	_____	_____	_____	_____
How I spend my money	_____	_____	_____	_____
How I look at sex	_____	_____	_____	_____
What I think of cheating to get a better grade	_____	_____	_____	_____
What I think of God and Christ	_____	_____	_____	_____
Growing toward a more real and warm personal relationship to Christ	_____	_____	_____	_____
Using my Bible more and praying more	_____	_____	_____	_____
My attitude toward work	_____	_____	_____	_____
My attitude toward my parents	_____	_____	_____	_____

Go back over the checklist and see just where your "peer group" is really influencing you. A person's "peer group" is the "crowd" to whose tune he really marches. Your peers are your "equals"—people who have something in common with you such as being students in the same high school, being in the same youth group at church, etc. Keep in mind, too, that there are possibly different peer groups that affect your life —perhaps one at school and another group in your church. Be scathingly honest with yourself when it comes to judging how much your peer group really influences you. It isn't necessarily wrong to be influenced by your peer group in certain areas. The question you have to ask yourself is: "Does my peer group influence me or does it completely dominate and control me?" Even more to the point: "Would I be willing to buck my peer group to strike off in another direction or do something completely against the ideas and wishes of the crowd because I had a personal conviction that disagreed with theirs?"

Romans 12:2 talks about being a different person in all you do and think. Can you look back on your life over the last six to twelve months and think about how you are becoming a new and different person with a fresh newness in all that you do and think? Why not look at several big areas: attitudes toward family; attitudes toward schoolwork or other responsibilities; attitudes toward minority groups; attitudes toward law enforcement agencies, attitudes toward government; attitudes toward the church; attitudes toward my pastor and other church leaders; attitudes toward Christ.

"... it is better to suffer for doing good than for doing wrong!" I Peter 3:17

SOME PEOPLE ARE MISSION IMPOSSIBLE!

"That guy really bugs me!"

"Oh, her? A born loser!"

"Yes, they're both real cold fish and they have such a condescending attitude to go along with it."

We all know these types. Some of them come through as overbearing, conceited slobs. Others seem to be the sly "never quite know what they're thinking" sneaks. Others are just plain obnoxious, unfriendly, and you would swear at times "unhuman."

They are "mission impossible." They come in all shapes, sizes and degrees of unlovableness. What makes them "mission impossible" is that the Bible teaches us to love one another, turn the other cheek, pray for those who kick you in the teeth, etc. And so we're left feeling a little bit frustrated. On one hand, we know that if being a Christian means anything, it means reaching out to others with God's love because we have experienced it ourselves. On the other hand, we find ourselves wanting to "keep our egos intact." It's the desire to be something more than a doormat, and it's built into most people. And the conflict comes for most of us when we make the sad but all too true discovery that we just can't get along with everyone. We just can't love everyone in the way the Bible seems to tell us to. This is a natural "ego defense mechanism" that gets out of hand even when we know that lashing back isn't really the right thing to do. We do it anyway because this something in us demands satisfaction. As Violet says in the cartoon, "I had to hit him quick . . . he was beginning to make sense."

And so, if you're a follower of Christ, what do you do? It might help, at least, to face the cold, hard facts: there are people who are bound to bug you. At the same time, face another colder and even harder fact: there are people whom *you* bug—yes, even sweet, intelligent, personable, "wouldn't hurt a fly" you. It's part of the human experience to grate on one another a little here and there. Perhaps that's why the Bible talks so much about love. Love is the oil that keeps the friction from becoming intolerable.

The apostle Peter was really talking about the "oil of love" when he wrote his first letter to the Christian Jews who had been scattered from one end of the known civilized world to the other for their beliefs. He gave them a lot of practical advice

on taking the lumps that people were handing out and doing it graciously and lovingly. For example . . .

Your assignment
(if you choose to accept it) . . .

"And now this word to all of you: You should be like one big happy family, full of sympathy toward each other, loving one another with tender hearts and humble minds. Don't repay evil for evil. Don't snap back at those who say unkind things about you. Instead, pray for God's help for them, for we are to be kind to others, and God will bless us for it.

"If you want a happy, good life, keep control of your tongue, and guard your lips from telling lies. Turn away from evil and do good. Try to live in peace even if you must run after it to catch and hold it! For the Lord is watching His children, listening to their prayers; but the Lord's face is hard against those who do evil.

"Usually no one will hurt you for wanting to do good. But even if they should, you are to be envied, for God will reward you for it. Quietly trust yourself to Christ your Lord and if anybody asks why you believe as you do, be ready to tell him, and do it in a gentle and respectful way.

"Do what is right; then if men speak against you, calling you evil names, they will become ashamed of themselves for falsely accusing you when you have only done what is good. Remember, if God wants you to suffer, it is better to suffer for doing good than for doing wrong! Christ also suffered. He died once for the sins of all us guilty sinners, although He Himself was innocent of any sin at any time, that He might bring us safely home to God. But though His body died, His spirit lived on" (I Pet. 3:8–18—*Living New Testament, Paraphrased*).

Fight, switch,
compromise or ???

At first glance, what Peter writes doesn't seem to have an awful lot to do with the daily nitty-gritty we face in the 1970's. Peter was writing his letter to people who were on the run because Nero had to find somebody for a scapegoat after Rome burned down in A.D. 64. The Jewish Christians were persecuted, hounded, scattered everywhere, as Peter says in the first verse of I Peter. They were really "under the gun." To say you were a Christian in Roman society in the first century was sort of like admitting you are a member of CORE at a meeting of the Ku Klux Klan. Today—in the Western world at least—few Christians are hounded, persecuted and killed for their faith. Actually, the "opposition" is much more subtle. The "persecution" is far more clever. But the opposition and the hostility toward the claims of Christ is still there. And so, perhaps Peter does have something to say to us here because what he talks about can be used by the sophisticated 20th century Christian whether he lives in the suburbs, the farmlands, or the inner city. The secrets to getting along with people really haven't changed much since Peter's day, and that's really what he's talking about here as he gives his Christian friends some "friendly advice."

The first thing that Peter makes clear is that the Christians should really stick together—be one big happy family, so to speak. This is the theme all the way through the New Testament. And, let's face it . . . plenty of the "mission impossible people" that a Christian runs into head-on are right in his own church and are members of the body of Christ themselves.

And so, Peter suggests that the Christian brothers should really try to be just that. They ought to first of all love one another and not put each other down. And then Peter goes on to deal with this problem of getting persecuted by the "outside establishment." Rule number one is don't slash back, repaying a chop with another chop. The easiest thing in the world to do is to "go to war." The hardest thing to do is to keep your cool and try to search out a logical rational solution to a disagreement or grievance or whatever the trouble might be.

In verse 10 Peter deals with that most unruly part of our body—our tongue. Too many people—and there are plenty of Christians among them—let their tongue go full speed before putting it into gear with their brain. They talk first, think (and pay) later. And—face the music—a lot of people, including Christians, tell lies. Of course, they don't tell too many big black, bold lies. They tell little "white ones," the little half-truths, the little innuendos, or that best and most comfortable approach to lying of all—not saying anything because "He didn't ask me that."

Peter puts it plainly. The Christian is to turn away from vengeance, gossip, and the countless other evil traps that are just waiting there to be jumped into. The Christian is to try to live in peace, even if he has to run after it to catch it and hold it.

Peter isn't saying that all the Christians should sneak around like a bunch of church mice at a cat convention, never letting people know how they really feel. It isn't a case of keeping your mouth shut because you're afraid you would offend someone if you breathe heavily. The key is in v. 15—just trust yourself to Christ, and when someone asks you why you believe as you do, be ready to tell them in a gentle and respectful way. It seems that too many of Christ's disciples fall into one of two major groups: the "silent service" who glide through their daily routines, keeping their true identity better hidden than any double agent ever could. Or there is that elite group of Christian commandos—the "shock troops" who let everybody know where they stand and lay most people out in the process. For example, in the following open-end story you have a fellow named Tom telling you his problems. Tom isn't real (or is he?) but his problem is definitely real. Perhaps in analyzing Tom's mistakes, you can find some better ways for carrying out "mission impossible"—loving those who don't seem so lovely to you and perhaps becoming a little more lovable to those who see you as something less than Mr. Wonderful or Miss Swell Gal.

"If They're All Like Your Buddy, Forget It!"

I knew Gordon didn't like either Rich or me, but especially me. Rich was my buddy and we had only been at Southeast High for a couple of weeks now. I decided to join the staff of the school paper, and Gordon was on the staff too. Guess that's why he didn't take to me.

Anyway, Rich and I were going down the hall to

the cafeteria when Gordon sort of swung by and asked us if we were going to the Senior Holiday Dance. I guess he was trying to test us because anybody could tell by our lives we were different.

Well, Rich shook his head, but didn't say anything. That was Rich—the quiet type. Why couldn't he pry open his lower jaw long enough to let people know how he felt about things like dances?

"Not me," I said, wagging my head. "I am a Christian and I don't believe in dancing. Since I have accepted Christ as my Saviour, I don't feel it's right . . ."

Gordon started laughing so hard I felt like clobbering him good. He made a sneering comment and then left.

Rich and I didn't talk too much during lunch. I was disgusted with him for not taking a definite stand—especially since we'd talked about this very thing before coming to Southeast High. From the way he had reacted to Gordon's question, I was beginning to wonder if he would be finking out on me.

We were just finishing dessert when this guy came along. Rich seemed to know him and introduced him to me as Dan Edwards. Rich seemed to know quite a bunch of people already. After talking a while, Dan said, "Look, guys, why don't we get a bunch of fellows together and all go down to the beach Sunday morning." He looked expectantly at me.

"Sorry," I said loud enough for those at the next table to hear, "but I'm a Christian and I believe in going to church on Sunday morning. All of you should be in church too." From the way he looked at me, it was obvious that Dan got the message. He turned to Rich, "How about you?"

Rich grinned at him. "I'd rather not go on a Sunday morning, but I need some exercise. How about my buddy and me challenging you and whomever you want to a couple of sets of tennis after school?"

"Sounds good," Dan agreed. "I didn't know you guys played tennis."

"We're pretty rusty," Rich admitted, "but you might get a few laughs out of it."

So we played tennis after school and got licked, naturally. Much to our surprise, Dan had brought Gordon, of all people. Naturally, he made a few digs at us—something about the two saints. Rich didn't do anything, but I gave Gordon a dirty look to let him know it wasn't appreciated.

After we were through playing, Gordon started telling a shady story just to see what we'd do. I steamed. But Rich, instead of putting Gordon in his place, shuffled off in the middle of the joke to collect the stray tennis balls.

Well, that left me holding the bag again. I interrupted Gordon. "Listen," I fumed, "Watch who you're talking to. *We* don't listen to that kind of trash. Lay off the smut when you're around us."

I really gave it to him, and of course I could have guessed his response. Called me Saint Thomas and a few other not-so-nice names, Gordon walked off. I figured on them acting that way, but what I hadn't expected was Rich walking away by himself. Guess he was embarrassed for not standing up to them like I had.

Since Dan had acted a little more civil than Gordon, I decided to invite him to church. I did the next day and he turned me down, but I figured I'd keep on asking. As for Gordon, he never had a decent thing to say when I'd see him up in the newspaper office, so I just ignored him.

On Sunday, when I was in church standing at the door waiting for the other kids to come, the door opened and in walked Rich with Dan! Talk about shocked—I couldn't believe Dan would actually come, and why would he come with Rich but not with me? Then I even heard Dan whisper to Rich as they saw me, "If they're all like your buddy, this is my last Sunday!"

I couldn't shake those words. They kept coming back to me all through the service. What had I done wrong? I was really shook up because I thought all along that I was doing a better job at being a Christian witness than Rich. How else should I act? Next thing you'd know, Rich would probably have Gordon in church. But what about me? Why couldn't I get along better with Gordon?*

What should Tom do?

If you were going to tell "Saint Thomas" what he was obviously doing wrong, what would you say? Why can't he get along better with Gordon?

If Tom wanted to change, what would you suggest? What are some pointers from the lesson that you could help him apply? Could you give Tom any ideas on how to act the next time he sees Gor-

*Adapted from a story by Larry D. Peabody in *Fourteen for Teens,* pp. 14–17.

don in order to start building a new and different relationship with him?

Why do you think Rich was successful in getting Dan to church? Do you agree with Rich's keeping quiet? Are there times when you should speak up?

WHAT CAN YOU DO?

Getting along with other people—particularly the "mission impossibles"—depends basically on your attitude toward them. Take the "Are you a mission impossible?" quiz on page 104. Check the column that most nearly identifies your attitude regarding each of the quiz questions. Keep in mind as you take this quiz that while some people are "mission impossible" to you, you are "mission impossible" to some people, too!

*　　*　　*

The challenge to communicate more clearly is an important part of learning to get along with difficult people or learning to be less difficult to get along with yourself. Try the following experiment—first with a friend with whom you communicate fairly easily, and then—in the right time and place—suggest this exercise with someone that you find difficult to like or talk to:

This exercise has only one rule—each person can state his viewpoint or ideas only after he has first restated the other person's ideas and feelings accurately and to that person's satisfaction.

The idea here is that each person in the conversation is trying to be sure that he heard what the other person said and that he can restate what the other person said accurately and to that person's satisfaction. Then, he can go on to make his own comment or observation. Then the other person can restate that observation and make another observation of his own in turn and so on.

This exercise might be a good one to try with parents, but it's particularly effective with anyone as long as both parties obey the rules. It may take a little longer to converse this way, but a lot more can be achieved in the long run.

AM I A "MISSION IMPOSSIBLE"?

	A FEW PEOPLE	SOME PEOPLE	MANY PEOPLE
Do others see me as a trustworthy person—somebody they can depend on to not be phony?	——	——	——
Do I express myself to others in a way that communicates to them who I really am? In other words, is it really me talking, or am I playing some kind of role because I am afraid or insecure or doing what I think people expect me to do?	——	——	——
Do I like other people easily? Do I enter into personal, positive relationships with others quickly in which I care for, like and respect other people?	——	——	——
Do I tend to depend on other people? That is, do I need other people to help me make up my mind about just about everything —or am I more of an independent person?	——	——	——
Am I willing to let other people be separate and independent—to be themselves—or do I want them to conform to my ideas and thinking?	——	——	——
Do I find it easy to understand other people—to put myself in their shoes?	——	——	——
Do I accept other people for what or who they are, or do I enter into relationships with people on certain conditions that they treat me right, please me, etc.?	——	——	——
Do I come on too strong for people? Do I threaten them, irritate them, make them want to "fight back"?	——	——	——
Do I make quick judgments on people — categorizing or pigeonholing them and treating them accordingly?	——	——	——
Can I see other people as persons who are in a growth process just as I am? Do I always see them with potential, or do I tend to see them as "hopeless cases" who can't possibly change from what they have been in the past?	——	——	——

"... it isn't enough just to have faith ..." James 2:17

I'M A GOOD MAN (I THINK)

"Snoopy looks kind of cold, doesn't he?" says Charlie Brown to Linus as the two of them trudge through the snow bundled up in warm clothes and spy the shivering Snoopy lying on the ground looking forlorn and slightly frozen.

"I'll say he does," says Linus. "Maybe we'd better go over, and comfort him."

"Be of good cheer, Snoopy," says Linus to the shivering Snoopy.

"Yes, be of good cheer," chimes in Charlie Brown. And the last frame in the episode shows Charlie and Linus trudging off with Snoopy sitting there, still shivering, with a question mark over his head. (See cartoon next page.)

The "moral" of this Peanuts "parable" is clear, but it is amazing how many Christians have missed

it. There is, in fact, a concentrated effort on the part of society to let the Christian church know that it just isn't putting its money or its good works where its mouth is. Preoccupation with doctrine and theology just isn't making it these days. "Bringing people 'comfort' in the form of beautiful phrases and clever clichés" isn't impressing anyone—particularly those outside the Christian fold.

How can Christians prove to the world their faith is real? A man named James wrote a "nasty" letter to his fellow Christian believers and in it he clearly spells out how to "prove your faith is real." In fact, part of what James writes is the inspiration for Charles Schulz' cartoon on telling Snoopy to "warm up" by being of good cheer. Christians like to think that their faith in Christ makes them "good men," and so it does in one sense, because trusting Christ

106

makes you righteous in God's sight. But there is more to being a good man than being "justified by faith." James talks about the other side of the coin in the following fashion . . .

Believing is useless unless . . .

"Dear brothers, what's the use of saying that you have faith and are Christians if you aren't proving it by helping others? Will *that* kind of faith save anyone? If you have a friend who is in need of food and clothing, and you say to him, 'Well, good-bye and God bless you; stay warm and eat hearty,' and then don't give him clothes or food, what good does that do?

"So you see, it isn't enough just to have faith. You must also do good to prove that you have it. Faith that doesn't show itself by good works is no faith at all—it is dead and useless. But someone may well argue, 'You say the way to God is by faith alone, plus nothing; well, I say that good works are important too, for without good works you can't prove whether you have faith or not; but anyone can see that I have faith by the way I act.'

"Are there still some among you who hold that 'only believing' is enough? Believing in one God? Well, remember that the devils believe this too—so strongly that they tremble in terror! Dear foolish man! When will you ever learn that 'believing' is useless without *doing* what God wants you to? Faith that does not result in good deeds is not real faith" (James 2:14–20—*Living New Testament, Paraphrased*).

Wanted: a faith you can see

One thing you have to keep remembering about James' letter. He isn't talking about earning a ticket to heaven by doing a lot of fine things. He's not talking about giving to charity, keeping the Ten Commandments, etc., as a means of being saved. James is talking to people who are professing Christians, people who claim that they have a relationship to God through believing in and accepting Christ.

James would never say that you could possibly "put yourself in shape" for God by keeping the rules and regulations. What James is talking about is putting one's faith into practice. James says you can show that your faith is real by helping others. Sound too simple? Look again at the cartoon on page 106.

As James says in verses 14–16, you don't tell a friend in need of food and clothes to feast on faith and keep warm with well-wishes.

Now, granted there aren't too many of us who actually know people who have no food or clothing. True, much of the world is starving and there is a great deal of poverty and hunger even in the affluent United States, but for the most part this isn't too close to home for a lot of us. There are, however, many ways to be "hungry and in need." In the "Peanuts" cartoon on the next page Charlie Brown lies helplessly on the ice trying desperately to get up but unable to move because his mother has him so heavily bundled up against the cold that he can't even bend his arms or legs. Lucy stands by him doing nothing except watching and she finally says, "I don't suppose there's anything I can do to help you?" As Charlie continues to struggle, Lucy suggests "How would it be if I hope for an early spring?"

(In a sequel to that cartoon, Snoopy comes along and does more than "hope for an early spring." He can't help Charlie Brown stand up, but he does do what he is able to do. He starts pushing Charlie along the ice with his nose!)

The "Peanuts" episode of Charlie Brown lying helplessly on the ice is a bit ridiculous, but it makes its point. We do have friends in need. They aren't lying on the ice too bundled up to bend their arms and legs so they can stand up, but people are "tied up" in many ways and they are in need. We meet people every day who "need food and clothes" of a different kind.

Many people (all people?) have emotional needs that are just as important as food and fashions. Have you ever wondered why that talkative person is so talkative? Do you think that it just might possibly be because he needs recognition and praise? Have you ever wondered why that certain girl acts as if she's "stuck-up"? Have you ever thought about looking underneath that frozen mask to find a person who is longing to be able to get over her shyness and fear of having to talk to people she doesn't know very well?

And what about the "losers"—the people who "just don't make it" with the "in" group (or with the "out" group, for that matter). It's not that they are so particularly obnoxious, they are just not much fun to have around. There just isn't much future in giving them the time of day. How does a Christian prove his faith by his works when one of the losers comes around? That's the big question in the following open-end story. How would you plug *this* open end? The "right answer" is obvious. But your real answer might be something else. It's worth thinking about . . .

Nobody Loves a Loser

Shirley sat in church listening to Pastor Davison's morning sermon from James, the second chapter. Her mind had been wandering and she had yawned about five times during the sermon because she had stayed up late the night before. The words sounded familiar. She had heard them a dozen times before.

She glanced at her watch, and if her thoughts could have been heard, a loud "Ho, hum" would have jolted those sitting three pews away. Fifteen whole minutes yet to go. She straightened up and looked again at Pastor Davison. Except she caught his words this time. "Is *your* faith dead?" The words seemed to fit her mood. *She* certainly felt lifeless. But what about her faith? Was that dead too?

She began to think. How does a person's faith get dead? She had been a Christian since she was very little. It seemed that she had always been a part of the church program. She faithfully attended church and took part in most of the youth activities. The group had sung in the old folks' home and gone canvassing in the neighborhood to invite new people to their church. She had done a lot of things like that with the young people. It seemed she certainly had done her share of good works for the Lord.

Shirley would have loved to have dropped the whole subject right there. If works were any indication of her faith, she must have quite a bit of faith stored up. But the word *dead* was kind of scary. The pastor kept repeating "Faith without works is dead."

Well, it was ridiculous to imagine her own faith in Jesus Christ as being dead. Look, she didn't go to movies or to school dances. She read her Bible and goodness knows, she tried to witness—at least she sneaked a few tracts into her unsaved friends' books once or twice. And so, with a satisfied smile, Shirley bowed her head as the closing prayer was said.

After the service she tried to bolt out of there because Anna Mae was coming toward her, and she didn't care to talk to her—not today anyway. Anna Mae was a big loser who wore thick glasses and talked kind of funny. She never really fit into their group. And once you said "Hi" to her she would corner you and talk to you, and you never could get rid of her. She would tell all her troubles, and the average person just didn't have time for that.

So Shirley pretended not to notice Anna Mae and kept her eyes straight ahead to the door. By ducking around old Mr. Gray, she managed to leave the girl behind. She quickly shook Pastor Davison's hand, said it was a nice sermon and hurried to the parking lot where the other kids usually congregated.

Out in the parking lot the usual gang gathered to chew the fat. Tim the leader tried to get the kids to make final plans for the big youth retreat they were going to next weekend. "Has everybody turned in their money?" he called out. He read off the names of those going.

Then someone yelled out, "Hey, that's six girls and six guys." A big laugh went up from the group.

Shirley joined in laughing. Their youth group was really a lot of fun. You certainly couldn't call them dead or anything like that.

Just then she looked over at the church. Anna Mae was coming out the door. She nearly tripped and fell on the last step. The other kids happened to look then, too, and someone said, "Clumsy Anna Mae again."

Shirley heard some adults asking her if she was all right. She said "yes" and began walking home. Then she turned and looked directly at Shirley.

For the first time, Shirley caught something in Anna Mae's look. It was a kind of sad and lonely look. She had never taken the time to notice before, but now Anna Mae seemed like a real person, one who needed friends and understanding and fun just as she did. She shouldn't have avoided her right after church. That was wrong. The thought entered her mind to go speak to her now. Maybe she should be invited to the retreat.

But why should she be the one to go invite her? The other kids would tease her and accuse her of spoiling their fun by creating an awkward situation. Anna Mae would make an odd number—and a loser at that. "But what *are* Christian works?" Shirley questioned as she thought of the morning service.

What should she do about this? How could she bring it up to the group without sounding like she was trying to be a saint? It wasn't her style to be a leader in things like this. She usually went along with what others decided. It's too hard to step out all by yourself and tell everybody else they're wrong, that they aren't treating someone right. All of them, like her, usually just said hello to Anna Mae and that was it. Oh, maybe they pretended to be interested and humored her a little, but that was all. "What will they think if I start acting real interested in Anna Mae?"

"Hey, Shirl," someone yelled, "why ya so quiet today?"

What should Shirley do?

Since it is not so much a question of what Shirley is *supposed* to do, what is her real problem?

How can Shirley avoid being phony to Anna Mae if she tries to "treat her right"?

Why is it so difficult to be genuinely interested in

some people? Is it just because they are "losers" or "the unlikable type," or is there something in us that holds us back?

How far should Shirley go with Anna Mae? If you were Shirley, would you invite her to the retreat? If you did invite her, would that settle the matter? Would that be all you would have to do to "prove your faith by your works?"

What are some positive steps that you can take personally to keep yourself or any groups you are in from becoming clannish and cliquish?

WHAT CAN YOU DO?

On the following page are some of the problems that James pinpoints in his letter. Go through them and give yourself a "faith physical" to see how spiritually healthy you really are. Check to see if these problems affect you a lot, sometimes, or hardly ever. Also be sure to make notations in the "Especially when . . ." column to pinpoint just when you do get angry, critical, jealous, etc. In this way you can start pinpointing certain people and certain situations that are particularly hard for you to handle and you can start asking God to help you deal with these.

Take a pencil and paper and write down three ways you plan to "prove your faith by your works" in the next 24 hours. Perhaps all you really need to write is "I am willing to prove my faith by my works," and see how long it takes to have something come up to give you the opportunity.

CHECKLIST FROM JAMES

PROBLEM	A LOT	SOME-TIMES	HARDLY EVER	ESPECIALLY WHEN . . .
1. Anger (James 1:20)	___	___	___	___
2. Sharp Tongue (James 1:26)	___	___	___	___
3. Showing Favoritism (James 2:1)	___	___	___	___
4. Critical (James 3:1)	___	___	___	___
5. Bragging (James 3:13)	___	___	___	___
6. Being Phony (James 3:14)	___	___	___	___
7. Jealousy (James 3:16)	___	___	___	___
8. Fighting (James 4:1)	___	___	___	___
9. Want only things that give pleasure (James 4:3)	___	___	___	___
10. Loving the world (James 4:4)	___	___	___	___
11. Pride (James 4:6)	___	___	___	___
12. Not sorry for wrong-doings (James 4:9)	___	___	___	___
13. Knowing right but not doing it (James 4:17)	___	___	___	___
14. Grumbling (griping) (James 5:9)	___	___	___	___

CHAPTER 10

"Honor your father and mother . . ." Ephesians 6:2

LIVING AT
GENERATION GAP

"Linda, how could you possibly do what you did? Stay out all night and sleep with a married man . . ."

"You need something that'll wake you up, young lady. Get your dog and follow me."

Linda's father led the way into the backyard carrying a .22 caliber revolver. About 100 yards from the house, he loaded the gun and handed it to Linda.

"Now you shoot your dog as punishment for what you've done to disgrace us. But before you do it, dig a grave for him and think about it."

Linda dug the shallow grave and then her father handed her the gun. "Just pull the hammer back and pull the trigger," was all he said. And then he walked away leaving Linda with her mother holding the dog. Linda pointed the pistol at her favorite pet, and then she moved the gun away. Before her mother knew what was happening, she had placed the pistol to her own head and fired.

"My God, my God!" screamed Linda's mother, "She shot herself!"

The ambulance arrived and Linda was rushed to the hospital, but there was little doctors could do. She died the next morning. Police reported that no charges could be filed against Linda's parents, except possibly "cruelty to animals." But their grief-stricken remorse was punishment enough. The "generation gap" in Linda's home resulted in the ultimate tragedy.*

The "generation gap" that exists in many homes between parents and their children doesn't usually end as tragically as it did for Linda. But that gap exists and it seems to be growing wider by the minute. So wide did the gap become by 1969 that CBS television network devoted a three-part series of one-hour programs to a special report called "Generations Apart," a study of the generation gap as it exists in the United States and other countries of the world.

Ninety-five percent of all the people interviewed in this special CBS survey—adults and youth—believed that there definitely is a generation gap and 25 percent of the young people who were interviewed, believed that gap was very large. In some homes the gap doesn't get a whole lot larger than

*Based on an actual news report in the *Los Angeles Times*, February 7, 1968.

some good loud griping because "they won't let me use the car," or "they never trust me," or "they keep treating me like a little kid. All they want me to do is get good grades, keep my nose clean and make them proud of me." In other homes the gap gets wider and we have anything from juvenile delinquency to dropping out to join the hippie movement through the teen-age underground.

And, the generation gap hasn't skipped Chistian homes, either. In fact, because homes are Christian, the gap often gets wider than ever because parents who have values firmly rooted in traditional religious concepts and Biblical teachings are often overly rigid in trying to help their sons and daughters "shape up and live spiritual lives."

What exactly is the problem? Ask the young people and they'll tell you it's "their fault," meaning mother and dad. Ask mother and dad, and they'll tell you that their children are just not "toeing the mark and taking their share of the responsibility and growing up as they should." What does the Bible say? Is there some answer in Scripture that everybody is missing? As in many problems, Scripture doesn't give some pat answer, but the principles are there for all to use if they want to . . .

If you honor mom and dad . . .

"Children, obey your parents; this is the right thing to do because God has placed them in authority over you. Honor your father and mother. This is the first of God's Ten Commandments that ends with a promise. And this is the promise: that if you honor your father and mother, yours will be a long life, full of blessing.

118

"And now a word to you parents. Don't keep on scolding and nagging your children, making them angry and resentful. Rather, bring them up with the loving discipline the Lord Himself approves, with suggestions and godly advice" (Eph. 6:1-4—*Living New Testament, Paraphrased*).

Crossing generation gap

In the first few verses of this passage, the writer, Paul the apostle, seems to be all on the side of the adults. After all, "Honor your father and mother" is pretty plain talk. And, it's true that a lot of parents like to wave this little red flag under the noses of their children as a form of "spiritual blackmail" to get them to shape up.

It seems to many teen-agers that the parents have all the fire-power because they can quote that fifth commandment, "Honor your father and mother" (Exod. 20:12). It almost looks like the Bible joins in a giant conspiracy of adults against children in order to "keep them in line."

But, as is often the case, first glance at what Scripture is saying is not usually enough, especially if you're looking at the problem with certain emotional blinders on. It's true that the fifth commandment teaches, "Honor your father and your mother, that your days may be long in the land which the Lord your God gives you" (Exod. 20:12). But note that when Paul repeats this in Eph. 6:2 he adds that "This is the first of God's Ten Commandments that ends with a promise" (*Living New Testament*).

Now if all that Paul or any other Biblical writers were interested in was "keeping the kids under control," he would hardly worry about making them any promises or implying that there might be benefits involved in obedience to parents. But there *are* benefits. The reason the Bible teaches children to obey and honor their parents is because such obedience and such honor is the key to a loving relationship in the most basic institution that a society has —the family and the home.

To "honor someone" is to treat that person fairly, to treat him or her as you would want to be treated, in short, to be fair, to be honest, and to be loving. The Bible teaches parents to teach their children obedience. Without such obedience and such honor, a family cannot operate successfully or effectively on the human level, much less a spiritual level.

Without honor and obedience just about anything can happen, and it often does. In 1968 the newspaper reported a bizarre case. A teen-ager married a serviceman who was shipped to Alaska, while she remained behind to live with her parents in California. Over a period of 38 days the girl and her husband made 95 telephone calls to each other, all of them charged to her father's number! The bill came to $4,509.81! The telephone company placed a lien against the father's home, and he had to put it up for sale in order to pay the bill.

"You know, that $4,500 is more than half a year's pay for me," said the father. "I'm doing my best to hold on to my sense of humor."

You have to admit, children often cause a lot of grief for their parents. Some of it is financial, such as the $4,500 phone bill. A lot of it is emotional.

Sometimes it's legitimate grief. Other times it's really parental pride that is at stake.

In the "Peanuts" cartoon, Lucy symbolizes the typical attitude taken by many parents. "Why should you care if I have opinions or personality or character?" asks Linus.

"Because if you don't have any character, it's a reflection on me!" responds Lucy in typical motherly fashion.

The "reflection on them" is what prompted Linda's parents to demand that she take her dog out and shoot him after Linda had admitted that she'd been out all night, sleeping with a married man. When parents take advantage of Scriptural teaching to "honor your father and your mother" they forget that Scripture always has a balance. In that same passage in Ephesians 6 Paul also says "And now a word to you parents. Don't keep on scolding and nagging your children, making them angry and resentful. Rather, bring them up with the loving discipline the Lord Himself approves, with suggestions and godly advice" (Eph. 6:4–*Living New Testament*).

This hardly sounds like it advises having your daughter shoot her dog if she disobeys you or causes you embarrassment or grief. In Colossians, Paul says much the same thing: "Fathers, don't scold your children so much that they become discouraged and quit trying" (Col. 3:21–*Living New Testament*). Linda "quit trying" in a drastic way. Instead of shooting her dog, she put the gun to her own head and pulled the trigger. In one final, desperate defiance of her parents' demands and what she saw as dictatorial tyranny, Linda took her own life and left her parents shattered and grieving with guilt and remorse.

Few teen-agers go as far as Linda did, but many take certain steps to demonstrate their anger, their resentfulness and the fact that they are discouraged and have given up.

"You just can't talk to my parents," is a familiar line. "They talk like they know it all, that they have been there and that I will grow up and see how right they are."

And so, there is responsibility on both sides, and both sides are failing to meet that responsibility. Teen-agers blame the parents and parents blame the teen-agers. The generation gap seems to grow wider. So what's to be done? Is the whole thing a standoff? Is it true that adults, and parents in particular, are "hopeless" and that communication between the generations is out of the question? The teen-ager can see it that way if he wants to (and many of them do because they want to), but if he is interested in living as Christ wants him to live (and let's remember that when Christ uttered all of His teachings, He was "over 30") he will look for some positive solutions.

One thing the teen-ager should remember is that no matter how crabby or unreasonable or "out-of-it" his parents might be, his parents are acting out of love and concern. It may be misguided and misapplied in many cases, true, but it is still love and concern. And, let's not knock it, love and concern on any basis today is a welcome commodity.

In other words, the teen-ager has a lot going for him because his parents "want to do the right thing." The teen-ager with any brains at all can make this parental desire to do the right thing work for him. But he'll never get any results if he "demands better performance" from his parents.

In the past few years, student demonstrators, black militants, delegates to peace talks and summit meetings, etc., etc., have all been in the news with their "demands." The result of these demands is always the same—fear and/or fight from the side upon whom they are making the demands. Whenever you "demand" anything from someone, you put him on his guard, you "get his back up," you ask for trouble. To demand something tells the other person, "I really don't care whether you want to do what I say or not. I'm going to take what I want, get what I want and it really doesn't matter what you do. You don't really count, you are just something in my way and I am going to get you out of my way."

A far better approach than demanding that the other side see our viewpoint or meet our standards of behavior is to accept the other side for what they are and to try to work out a compromise situation that might even turn into understanding and empathy for one another.

For example, if teen-agers and parents really want to do something constructive about the "generation gap" they ought to recognize the smaller "sub-gaps" within the broad confines of the total picture of generations which seem to be very far apart on so many things.

For example, there's the *culture gap*. Today's teen-agers grew up in a technological society with such things as computers, transistors, television, etc., all of which were not available when their parents were children. Today's teen-agers are far better educated at their point of life than their parents were (and many of them are far better educated right now than their parents ever will be). The impact of television alone on the teen-age generation is still only fractionally understood.

Marshall McLuhan, the so-called prophet of communications in the 20th century, has explored the nature of the generation gap in terms of "hot" and "cool" communication. The old folks—the parents who grew up on newspaper and radio consumption, are what McLuhan terms "hot communicators." According to McLuhan, black print and rapid-fire radio delivery is hot communicating. The speaker attempts to keep the attention of his audience with a rapid-fire staccato presentation. This worked well through the 40's and up into the 50's.

Then television made its debut in 1948 and the tide turned toward cool communication—total involvement of the listener and the viewer as he watched the 21-inch screen and was "right there" living out the soap opera, watching the newscast as it happened on the spot, cheering with the crowds as they nominated a candidate for the presidency, etc., etc.

Today's teen-ager is much more tuned in to "cool communication." The line-upon-line linear presentation of ideas just doesn't grab him any more. He tunes it out, and that is exactly why he doesn't seem to listen when dad mounts his pulpit to deliver the weekly sermon on getting in on time. Dad can't understand why his son doesn't listen and just writes it off as rebellion and sheer mule-headedness. "And what are these kids coming to, anyway?"

And so, in the typical home, there are hot and cool communication lines, and these wires are often crossed. Mix this with the tremendously stepped-up pace of today's society, and you have the makings of real trouble and real trouble is what you have in many homes. The typical complaint by many parents is that their teen-agers don't live with them, they simply use the house as a "crash pad" where they drop in for meals and a few winks of sleep. The essence of "cool communication" is involvement and the trouble with too many families is that teen-agers are simply not involved with their parents and vice versa. Strangers live in the same house and communicate on a level that is one or two cuts above gutteral grunts and occasional screams of anger.

So what can a teen-ager do about this? He can try staying home a little more often. He can try talking to his parents and asking their opinion on certain questions. Parents love to be asked their opinion, and while they might preach a bit as they give it, the teen-ager might learn something about how to communicate with them—if he wants to.

Another "sub-gap" is the *honesty gap*. Again both sides are at fault. The parents are well-known for their hypocritical stance, telling their children to do one thing while their action speaks so much more loudly than their sermons. On the other side, the teen-ager gripes and carries on and often delivers speeches worthy of an Academy Award or at least an Emmy.

But what every teen-ager has to examine—deep within himself—is that while he thinks he has plenty of things to gripe about, he also has to think about just how well he is pulling his share of the load at home. Is he really a persecuted martyr as he would have everyone believe or is he giving the world a "snow job"? What about the responsibilities such as doing an adequate job of studying, being courteous, helping with the family chores (and even offering to help!)? The typical trap that most teen-agers fall into, (and most adults are in this trap too) is self-centeredness. As long as you go into a situation worrying only about how you see things and your own benefits and your ideas, you can expect nothing but opposition and disagreement from the other person. Self-centeredness is at the heart of the attitude that makes demands. Far better to come at it as the Bible teaches. Love doesn't make demands, it suggests, it requests, and it says "please" in manner as well as in word.

Finally, there is the *acceptance gap*. Both sides of the generation gap have plenty to work with here. Neither side is perfect, therefore the challenge is built-in. Both sides have to start accepting one another as something less than perfect. The teen-ager has come up through the childhood years and early in life he learned that his "almighty parents" were something less than perfect. He saw that his omnipotent, omniscient mother and father could make mistakes, that they don't always think too straight and they are far from consistent in what they say and what they do.

The parents, on the other hand, have been looking at their teen-ager ever since the cradle. They have "accepted his childishness" but now they feel that it is time that he should start "growing up a little and becoming more mature." Adults don't want to "accept teen-age manners" (or lack of same), teen-age hair styles, clothing, fads, tastes in music, entertainment, etc., etc., because they are a little "tired of waiting." It has been a long haul from the cradle to later adolescence. The parents are tired. They want some fruits for their labors, and they are, frankly, looking for a lot more than many teen-agers are capable of.

And so, both sides are far from perfect, and yet, both sides are going to have to live with something less than perfection if they want to close the generation gap. The Bible makes it clear that acceptance of others is not an award that we pass out to them because they "treat us right" or because they perform in just the way we want them to. The Golden Rule makes it clear that we should "Treat others as you want them to treat you" (Luke 6:31—*Living New Testament*).

The very heart of the Gospel is that God didn't exactly accept us because we treated Him so nicely. On the contrary, God accepted us when we deserved no acceptance whatsoever. In a family relationship, acceptance of each other is not an end product of a parent-child relationship. It should actually be the beginning. It is only through accepting one another that you can develop any kind of relationship with someone else. And so again, the teen-ager is left with the very real possibility that he should take the first step, as hard as that first step might be. So your father is a grump or an overworked, preoccupied bore. So your mother is a nag. So your parents don't trust you enough. So they are dictatorial and high-handed and "too strict."

So?

So, you have several choices. You can fight, and many teen-agers do. Or, you can switch—switch allegiance from your family to your peer group. Some teen-agers even switch addresses. There is a third alternative, however—you can accept. That doesn't mean that you resign yourself to life as a slave in a prison where your parents are the wardens. Keep in mind that they do want to do a good job and they do love you. Keep in mind that the Christian life is a life of growth and change.

If you are a Christian and your parents are Christians you have a tremendous reservoir of power available. It is possible for your home to be one in which the members of the family do "love one another." The trouble is that in so many Christian homes, as well as in too many churches and youth groups, Christians go at this business of loving one another in a passive way. They nod assent to the idea and then sit back and do so very little. But when you accept someone as he is, you love in an active way. As John says in I John 3:18, you love one another in deed and in truth, not just in words.

And even if a teen-ager comes from a home where the parents are not Christians and he is, he can still love them actively. He can still accept them just as he knows he has been accepted by God.

These "opportunities for acceptance" are just about limitless. In the everyday routine, a hundred different things come up that can cause disagreement, bitterness, arguing. There is this business of parents worrying about "How well is my teen-ager doing, because I am concerned about how he will make *me* look?" This could be the case in the following open-end story as George and his father have a "little chat" about the low grade George got on a biology test. George has no plans to be a biologist. Right now it's the furthest thing from his mind. But what George is planning to do seems to make little impression on his father. All his father knows is that George seems to goof off a lot and that he doesn't do enough studying. And so, father lays down the law. It's a familiar scene. Perhaps you've been there, and recently, at that. The question is, what can you do about it? Making demands won't work, so what will?

Stop the Treadmill
—I Want to Get Off!

"So I got a low mark in biology. I'm interested in going into social work. When am I ever going to dissect a frog once I get out of school?" George was bitter. He looked at his father, who was coldly folding his paper, as he fished for words.

"Don't get smart, young man. Don't give me all that nobility talk about being too busy helping solve the world's problems to come down to earth long enough to take care of your own problems."

"What do you expect? There's only so much time in one day. There are lots of things to do. All right —I goofed, but it wasn't a deliberate thing. You act like I'm just trying to spite you with deliberate low grades. It was just one of those things. I *do* try to keep my grades up. But you act like it was my only function in life to be a little drudge with the books so I can make you proud. Can't I be myself for a while?"

"If being yourself means falling down in your studies and spending too much time with your friends doing nothing—what kind of a person do you want to be?"

"Someone who isn't on a treadmill. Someone who is considered enough of an adult that I don't have to answer for every little thing that I do."

"Adults have privileges because they also have— and accept—responsibilities. I want you to be in every night this week by eight o'clock, so you can finish your studies and get a decent night's sleep."

What should George do?

Picture yourself in this scene. Would you stomp out of the room and stay out "past eight o'clock" that very night? Or would you come home on time but refuse to study?

Do you think that possibly George might be giving his dad a "snow job"? Maybe George is, to put it bluntly, lazy.

Do you think that George's father has too narrow an idea of his son's needs as a human being? Do you think that his father is over-reacting and that he is almost pressing the panic button because George won't get into the right college and be a credit to his family?

If you were George, what would you do about the eight o'clock curfew and what would you do about trying to improve the relationship between yourself and your father?

WHAT CAN YOU DO?

Use the rating scale on p. 133 to evaluate certain areas of life and just where you see more acceptance is needed on your part or on the part of your parents. If you feel that things are fairly well balanced, you will want to check the "3." If you think that your parents are more the cause of disagreements in a certain area, you will want to check the "4" or the "5." But, if you think that possibly you need to "shape up" in certain areas to help bring about more peace and tranquility, then you will want to check the "1" or the "2."

After completing the rating scale, work on areas where you honestly feel that you need to do more "obeying." As for the areas where you have honestly felt that your parents are more the cause of trouble, think about ways that you can accept their attitudes and actions and hopefully get them to change because you can make them see that you want to do the right thing and please them in these areas. As the Scriptures teach, "a soft answer [turns] away wrath," and to paraphrase this same idea on a reverse basis: "A demand usually means war."

* * *

Write a brief letter to your mother or dad concerning how you feel about the generation gap. If you have good relations with your parents, thank them for this and express your gratitude that the generation gap is not a problem in your home. If you aren't having such good relations, express your concern and say that you want to help close this gap every way you can. If possible, suggest some practical steps that you want to take to improve the situation. For example, you may know that your parents are bugged by your wanting to stay out too late, and so why not offer to get in earlier? Or perhaps your battleground is homework, such as George and his father in the open-end story. Why not offer to make a real effort to bear down harder on homework?

Perhaps this chapter didn't "turn you on" and you feel that your situation at home is as hopeless as ever. Perhaps you simply have no desire to "get in" in any area as far as your parents are concerned because you think they are all wrong and all wet and strictly out of it. If this is the case, face a very solemn fact, you are in bad shape.

If you can't see any hope for improving the situation between yourself and your mother and father, then you are going to have to come to grips with the quality of your relationship with your heavenly Father. Here is the real issue, in the final analysis. You can't love anyone else, and that includes your parents, unless you know and experience the love of God in Christ. All of the "practical suggestions" for getting along with parents are only possible as God enables you to put these suggestions into action. The trouble with a lot of Christian living is that it's going through "Christian motions" without any Christian power. Many a Christian is trying to drive the straight and narrow way, but he's out of gas and so he doesn't get anywhere. If this seems to be your situation, then pray—ask God to give you a new attitude and perhaps what you really need is to ask God to give you a new nature . . . one that makes you sure that your sins are forgiven because you've trusted Christ as your Saviour. It's one thing to try to drive the Christian highway without any gas. But some people actually try to drive it *without a car*, and this is difficult indeed.

GENERATION GAP AT MY HOUSE?

"Children, obey your parents; this is the right thing to do because God has placed them in authority over you" (Eph. 6:1—Living New Testament).	1	2	3	4	5	"And now a word to you parents. Don't keep on scolding and nagging . . ." (Eph. 6:4—Living New Testament).
Homework	—	—	—	—	—	
Curfew	—	—	—	—	—	
Dating	—	—	—	—	—	
The car	—	—	—	—	—	
Family chores	—	—	—	—	—	
Sex	—	—	—	—	—	
Friends	—	—	—	—	—	
Hairstyles	—	—	—	—	—	
Clothing styles	—	—	—	—	—	
Money	—	—	—	—	—	
Television	—	—	—	—	—	
Films	—	—	—	—	—	
Dances	—	—	—	—	—	
Reading matter	—	—	—	—	—	
Time at home	—	—	—	—	—	
Rock music	—	—	—	—	—	

CHAPTER 11

"Don't worry about anything . . . tell God your needs . . ."
Philippians 4:6

SURVIVAL IN THE PRESSURE COOKER

One of the continuing themes in the "Peanuts" cartoon strip is "Linus and his blanket." Linus has "gotta have that security blanket!" no matter what happens.

In one classic "blanket adventure" we see Linus under severe pressure. He is mumbling something about hating Mondays and Lucy is telling him to relax, but how can Linus relax when his blanket is in the wash!

Linus proceeds to get the "blanket D.T.'s." He can't breathe, the walls are closing in. Somebody has to help him. Lucy dashes for the dryer and comes running back with the blanket "just in time." Linus is saved, content with his blanket, and Lucy pronounces her benediction on the case by saying that in medical circles this is known as a "spiritual tourniquet." (See cartoon on next page.)

We all laugh at Linus and his blanket, but we

OH, HOW I HATE MONDAYS!

RELAX!

HOW CAN I RELAX WITH MY BLANKET IN THE WASH? WHY DOES SHE HAVE TO WASH IT ANYWAY?! IT WASN'T VERY DIRTY!

I GOTTA HAVE THAT BLANKET!

I CAN'T BREATHE! THE WALLS ARE CLOSING IN ON ME! I'M GETTING WEAK! GASP - GASP - HELP ME, SOMEBODY! HELP ME!!!

AAAUGHH!

HOLD ON! HERE IT COMES!

FROM THE WASHER TO THE DRYER TO YOU!

SAVED!

SIGH!

I GUESS HE'LL BE ALL RIGHT NOW...

IN MEDICAL CIRCLES THAT IS KNOWN AS THE APPLICATION OF A SPIRITUAL TOURNIQUET!

laugh because there is a very real truth here. We have all known small children who have had to have their blankets, too (ourselves included). And, as we get older, we continue to need our "security blankets," only they take different forms. The need for security is basic in any human being, no matter what his age.

Some of us find security in the crowd—the "in" group, those overruling masters of our lives called our peers. Others find security in their ability to achieve their athletic prowess or their physical appearance—their clothes, their cars, their looks, etc. And, some people turn to other things for security —alcohol, tobacco, drugs. In modern day society, the pace and the pressure are so fast and so fierce that all of us have times when we feel like Linus. "I gotta have that blanket!"

Do Christians need security blankets? Well, in one way they do and in another way they don't. Christians like to point out that they don't need any "worldly security blankets." The idea is that your Christian faith makes you so sufficient you don't need the crowd or material things or success or drugs, etc., etc. And so, the Christian—especially the Christian teen-ager—learns how to "play the game." He learns what to say and what not to say when he is around parents, pastors, and other "straight types" who want him to be "no problem and very spiritual."

The result, of course, is that as far as church life is concerned, many a Christian young person feels very insecure because his experience is really only an act. At the same time, he tries to find his security in all those things that are supposedly "no-no's." The crowd *is* important. Looks, clothes, hairdos *are* important. Money and personality *are* important. Success, respect, having people nudge each other when you go by and look at you admiringly—this is "where it's at" and this is what really counts.

Interestingly enough, however, the Christian does have a "security blanket" that comes straight from God with no other trimmings attached. The best thing about this kind of blanket is that it gives the Christian far more ability and skill and power to handle the pressure cooker we call life. And the Christian doesn't ever have to worry about anyone "taking my blanket away" because this blanket can't be taken away *as long as you want it*. Really wanting this blanket is the only string attached . . .

"I can do everything God asks me to . . ."

"Always be full of joy in the Lord; I say it again, rejoice! Let everyone see that you are unselfish and considerate in all you do. Remember that the Lord is coming soon. Don't worry about anything; instead, pray about everything; tell God your needs and don't forget to thank Him for His answers. If you do this you will experience God's peace, which is far more wonderful than the human mind can understand. His peace will keep your thoughts and your hearts quiet and at rest as you trust in Christ Jesus.

"And now, brothers, as I close this letter let me say this one more thing: Fix your thoughts on what is true and good and right. Think about things that are pure and lovely, and dwell on the fine, good things in others. Think about all you can praise God for and be glad about. Keep putting into practice all you learned from me and saw me doing, and the God of peace will be with you.

"How grateful I am and how I praise the Lord that you are helping me again. I know you have always been anxious to send what you could, but for a while you didn't have the chance. Not that I was ever in need, for I have learned how to get along happily whether I have much or little. I know how to live on almost nothing or with everything. I have learned the secret of contentment in every situation, whether it be a full stomach or hunger, plenty or want; For I can do everything God asks me to with the help of Christ who gives me the strength and power" (Phil. 4:4–13—*Living New Testament*).

What price peace under pressure?

At the risk of sounding disrespectful and possibly even sacrilegious, what Paul writes in his letter to the Philippians sounds a bit like a man "on a trip." After all, wouldn't you have to be a bit "high" to start talking about being full of joy in the Lord no matter what? Isn't it a bit unrealistic to say "Don't worry about anything"? And, doesn't that line "I can do all things through Christ" sound like the same kind of delusions of grandeur that cause LSD takers to decide they are going to step out the fifth floor window for a breath of fresh air?

Is it really possible to be full of joy in the Lord and to always rejoice? Is it possible to never worry? What about this idea of praying about everything? What about peace? Can you have peace when pressure is closing in—when term papers are due, when finals are coming, when money is short, and your parents' tempers are even shorter?

Is peaceful rejoicing possible when you feel like a tiny blob in that sea of impersonal humanity known as your high school? Is it possible to rejoice as teachers look through you, past you, around you but never really *at* you or *into* you as they process you and your friends like so many IBM cards? It is no wonder that one student taped a sign on his back that went something like this: "I am a human being. Please do not fold, bend, staple or mutilate."

Paul the apostle thought it was possible, but then he didn't live in an impersonal, technological jungle full of computers, penthouses, and production-line schedules. No, Paul didn't write this letter under those circumstances. He was only in prison. He was a "guest" of Caesar's Praetorian guard, the crack troops that guarded the emperor himself. The only pressure on Paul was that he might lose his head at any moment—literally. (And tradition has it that he finally did.)

So, before we dismiss what Paul writes about rejoicing and having peace under pressure, we should take a look at what he does say and why he says it. Paul knew plenty about rejoicing when the heat was really on. Paul knew what he was talking about when he said "Don't worry about anything, but pray about everything." Paul was talking about something he had experienced. He wasn't giving out with theory from an air-conditioned ivory tower.

Paul had a "security blanket," all right; but it was the kind that never needed washing, that Snoopy couldn't possibly grab away, that grandma couldn't try to confiscate, that Lucy couldn't cut up with a pair of scissors to make flannelgraph figures. Paul's "security blanket" was Christ Himself, and in Christ Himself, Paul found plenty of reason to say that he could rejoice and have peace under pressure.

Paul practiced some of the soundest psychology there is. Note his specific suggestions for being able to be full of joy and rejoicing. He says "Let everyone see that you are unselfish and considerate in all [that] you do. Remember that the Lord is coming soon" (Phil. 4:5—*Living New Testament*) In other words, get your mind off yourself and on other people and *on* Jesus Christ.

In his book *Are You for Real?*, author Larry Richards includes a report by an Iowa girl who experienced terrible depression while a senior in high school. She wrote, "I couldn't quite make out the why of life. Usually I'm a very happy person, but I got to the point where happiness seemed a never-never thing I'd outgrown. About that time I heard a short devotional. It was on Psalm 37:4, 'Delight thyself in the Lord and He will give you the desires of your heart.' I was desperate enough to try anything, so the next two Sundays I spent quietly, no homework, not seeking my own pleasure, no T.V., devotions in the afternoon. The desire of my heart was to be happy and content. The Lord gave it to me showing how wonderfully He keeps His promises If we seek Him we even have what we DESIRE not just what we need!"*

Now check this out. The Scriptures say that God will give you the desires of your heart, and this is very true. Desire only those things that are selfish self-centered and strictly for your own benefit, and

Are You for Real?, Richards, p. 146.

you will gain exactly this—selfishness, self-centeredness, and complete frustration. The desire to know real peace in Christ and to know the peace that comes from thinking a little more of others and a little less of self will gain you feelings of joy and security that you didn't know were possible. Yes, it's very true, you do get what you desire.

Paul continues to make rash statements when he goes on to say, "Don't worry about anything." Some people put on a pretty good front here; they act as if "I couldn't care less." There are always the "cool ones" who appear unruffled even when the traffic cop is coming up to the window of the car, when the score is tied and they're at the free throw line with one plus one, when they're coming to the plate with a man on first and third, two out, and the score tied in the ninth. When the teacher pulls out a "surprise test." Yes, some people can "keep their cool" but does that mean that they aren't worried? Worry is a basic human emotion. You might call it "concern" but to say that "I never worry" is about as possible as to say "I hardly ever breathe."

So, what does Paul mean here? You get your clue in the next few words because he says that instead we should pray about everything. "Tell God your needs and don't forget to thank Him for His answers" (Phil. 4:6—*Living New Testament*).

More sound psychology here. Paul isn't saying that Christians never worry or never have any concerns. What Paul is saying is "take your worries and your concerns to God in prayer." What Paul is saying is "Don't dwell on your worries and anxieties. Do something about them. Tell God about it and thank Him for what He will do even before He seems to have done it." To be continually worried and anxious is to be insecure. But the Christian doesn't have to live like this because he has his own built-in security blanket. He has the Holy Spirit of Christ living in him and all he has to do is relax.

"But how can I relax? It's all very well to talk about relaxing, but if I flunk this final it means a 'D' in the course, and a 'D' in the course means getting turned down by the college that my folks want me in next fall." Yes, relaxing under pressure does seem like a useless thing to talk about, but note again that Paul's psychology is sound. He says "Tell God your needs."

A basic psychological principle is to allow people to "get things off their chests." A great deal of psychotherapy for highly disturbed mental patients involves only their talking while the psychotherapist listens attentively and understandingly. So, the principle holds just as true for the Christian. Praying is "telling God about it." Once you have told God about it, you have every reason to be able to relax. You've put the thing in His hands and you've taken the pressure off of your own back.

Does it sound mysterious? There is definitely an element of mystery. But it does work. It does work if God is real to you and not just an abstract idea in a list of dry and dusty doctrines. That's why Paul can write "If you do this [pray about it] you will experience God's peace, which is far more wonderful than the human mind can understand" (v. 7). This kind of peace, says Paul, keeps your mind and your heart quiet and at rest—*as you trust in Christ.*

Another personal experience recorded in Larry Richards' book *Are You for Real?* concerns a boy who was constantly worried about flunking his freshman year in college. He kept wondering if he was "really in the Lord's will." Finally, one of his teachers guided him to Prov. 3:5,6. "Trust in the Lord with all thine heart; and lean not unto thine own understanding. In all thy ways acknowledge him, and he shall direct thy paths." This freshman did this in prayer and God answered his prayer. He started sleeping better and doing better work in his classes. He realized that while he had to do his part, God would certainly come through at His end, *if* he really tuned in on God's wave length.* As the *Living Psalms and Proverbs, Paraphrased* puts it, "In everything you do, put God first, and He will direct you and crown your efforts with success."

Does it all still sound rather vague and mysterious? Perhaps Paul realized this because he went on to say "let me say this one more thing" (v. 8). Then he proceeded to follow up with some more sound psychology—to fix your thoughts, your ideas, on what is true, good, right, pure, lovely, fine. And, above all, "keep putting into practice all you learned from me" (v. 9).

In a way, Christianity is a paradox. You don't work to get on the team (Eph. 2:8,9). That is, you don't show up in training camp for "tryouts" and succeed in "surviving the cut" (Titus 3:5). You are accepted on the team on a completely different basis—your complete and open admittal that you

---

Are You for Real?, Richards, pp. 146, 147.

need to be on the team (Rom. 10:9,10). But once you "make the team," how you perform as a Chrisian in the so-called "game of life" depends entirely on how often you show up for practice (Eph. 2:10, John 15:1–7).

The reason a lot of Christians are fumbling the ball is that they are rusty, they are out of shape, they are undisciplined, untrained. In a word they are "flabby" and they wind up failures. They expect their coach* (Christ) to play the ball game for them. They expect Him to throw the blocks, make the tackles, catch the ball and grind out the yardage. They expect Him to fire across the third strike to win the ball game. They expect Him to get the hit and bring in the winning run.

But that isn't the way it works. Salvation in Christ is strictly of God. He does it all. Christian living is strictly something the Christian does as he allows Christ to work in and through him. The only way to allow Christ to work in and through you is to practice. Christian living takes discipline—not a slavish obedience to a lot of Mickey Mouse rules—but a determined attempt to allow God to change you and remake you from within. That changing and remolding can only come through practice. Any athlete or musician or speaker or teacher or craftsman—anyone will tell you that without practice you waste your time. One of the most superb examples of a well-conditioned athlete is Edward Villella, who, according to *Life* magazine, trains harder and demands more of his body (and gets more

---

*Apologies to all those who dislike comparing Christ to a coach, but the analogy must go on.

from his body) 52 weeks a year than any participant in amateur or professional sports. Is Villella a superstar of the baseball diamond, the gridiron? At 5'7½" it is doubtful that he would play center in the NBA. Soccer, perhaps, or maybe he is an underrated track standout?

Villella is none of these, and yet he combines the skills and stamina of all of these. *Villella is a ballet dancer with the New York City Ballet.* After every performance, Villella is soaked in sweat, gasping for breath, aching in every muscle, and completely exhausted. He soars bird-like through the air and actually hangs up there longer than it seems right for gravity to permit. As he makes one of his exits from the stage, he is flying through the air heading east and suddenly twists in mid-flight to face west as he disappears into the wings.

Villella's waist is 28 inches but his leg muscles are so fully developed that he has to buy 30-inch slacks. A nurse was once tending his twisted ankle and she noted a huge bulge in his thigh. She thought it was a broken bone, but actually it was solid muscle.

All-important to Villella before every performance is his warm-up. He stretches, probes, tests and coaxes every muscle in his body with every possible contortion from splits to stretches to bends of every kind.

"If the warm-up is right," he says, "the performance is a cinch. It's all downhill."*

There is a very real parallel here as far as Christian living is concerned. Too many Christians get

*See *Life* report on Villella, June 6, 1969, p. 48.

into demanding pressure situations, but they've had no warm-up. In fact, they've had no practice or workout of any kind. They wonder why they can't "show Christian love" or why they so quickly lose their temper or are so quickly frightened, frustrated. The answer is that they've had no practice—practice in prayer, practice in digging deep into the Scriptures—not to get in their chapter a day—but to find the vital and personal fellowship with Jesus Christ that is available for those who will ask, seek and knock.

Paul had learned the "secret of discipline and practice" in his Christian living. So when Paul wrote about rejoicing in any kind of situation, no matter how heavy the pressure, he knew from experience that it could be done. When he talked about not worrying about anything, he knew that he could turn his anxieties and his worries over to Christ in prayer. Paul could say without any twinge of doubt, "With the help of Him who empowers me, I feel up to *anything*" (Phil. 4:13—*Cotton Patch Version of St. Paul's Epistles*).

Paul wasn't self-sufficient, he was Christ-sufficient. Paul realized that you couldn't escape the pressure cooker of life unless you achieve one of two conditions—rigor mortis or schizophrenia. But Paul also realized that there is a way to control the pressure cooker. As long as that safety valve is bobbing up and down and the steam is escaping in correct amounts, the pressure cooker is actually something that is a positive force that can produce good and get a job done. That safety valve is prayer and the steam—the power—is Jesus Christ Himself!

In the following open-end story we find a girl who is facing a pressure-packed situation. Pressure is being applied by her mother and a doting teacher who wants to see her "make good." A schoolmate doesn't help matters any when he suggests a very obvious but highly questionable solution to her dilemma. What would you do if you were . . .

Half a Point from an "A," But . . .

"Sally, will you wait a minute after class? I want to talk with you," asked Mrs. Peters. After the class had left, Mrs. Peters continued. "Sally, I'm so very pleased with the work you are doing in English. I figured your grades last night and you are just short of an 'A' by only half a point. I do hope you will be able to study just a little bit harder for the final, and make that 'A.' That would please me so much. Since we go to the same church I'm very anxious for you to succeed."

"I'll certainly try my best," replied Sally.

"And, Sally, if you make an 'A' that means you will be eligible for the Literary Club. I would be so happy to place your name in nomination."

"I'll try! But I've got to go," Sally said, anxious to get away.

Bill was waiting outside the room for Sally. "What did she want?"

Sally sighed. "She told me I was a ½ point from an 'A.' She says I have to study harder. Teachers just never seem to realize that some of us are not 'A' students. Why can't parents and teachers realize that?"

"It would help," Bill added as they walked home.

"I'll bet my mother talked to her at church—she goes to the same church we do—because my mother said something last night about how proud she would be if I made the Literary Club."

"The Literary Club?" whispered Bill, astonished. "That's the cream!"

"It all adds up now," continued Sally. "Even my dad, the first time he has ever had time to help me, went through my class notes reviewing with me. He said he would ask one of the girls at the office to come in on Saturday and type them on cards for me. Can you imagine? Wait till they hear about my ½ point. Then they will really turn on the heat."

"It's a good thing you have the weekend to study," consoled Bill. "Look—there's your mother at the door, waiting for you!"

"Sally! I'm so happy and excited for you! Oh, hi, Bill." Sally's mother was bubbling with excitement. "Mrs. Peters phoned and told me about your 'A' and she even suggested that if you want to, you could go over to her place Sunday afternoon and she would review with you. I think . . ."

"Excuse me, but I'd better go on home," Bill said as he left.

Saturday and Sunday seemed to drag for Sally. It was one long hassle with her parents and their constant review. "Who wrote the 'Ode on a Grecian Urn'? Emily Dickinson is classed as what kind of poet?" and on and on.

It was nice to see Bill again Monday morning. "Hi, Sally! I suppose that you know it all by now?"

"I've got it all right here on the cards Dad had typed," answered Sally. "Sure wish it were in my brains instead."

"Why don't you just use them," Bill said, pointing to the cards.

"Use them?" queried Sally. "You mean use them to cheat from?"

"Sure. Why not? If an 'A' means so much to your parents and Mrs. Peters, why not? After all, there's not much justice in keeping a nice kid like you from an 'A' by a lousy ½ point. That's one of the things that rubs me about grading anyway. Why is her ½ point so important?"

"But Bill, I can't cheat!" Sally almost whispered it. "What if I got caught? What would my parents say?"

"What are they going to say if you don't get the 'A'?"

"Bill," Sally stopped dead in her tracks, "Tell me, do you cheat?"

A little smile crossed Bill's face and he tried to give a little titter, "Well, I wouldn't put it that way."

"I sure hope you don't! That would be a scandal. I can see it, 'Outstanding first baseman caught cheating! Wilson High's big hope for next year's conference title expelled!' "

"Cut the dramatics! No one has caught me yet, and they won't if you don't squeal!"

"Why, Bill Jenkins! I never thought . . ."

"Here's your room," Bill stopped her. "If I were you I would tuck those cards up my sweater sleeve. Think of it this way. You're not cheating for yourself. It's for your parents and their prestige, their pride and joy. It's for Mrs. Peters. It doesn't make any difference to you whether it is an 'A' or a 'B.' Does it? I've got to go or the coach will be mad if I'm late. Good luck!"

Sally entered the room, smiled at Mrs. Peters and dropped into her seat. She looked to see what Mrs. Peters was doing and slipped the cards into her sleeve . . .

What should Sally do?

Sally is under heavy pressure to cheat on an exam in order to get an "A." What are the main sources of this pressure? Her own ambition? Parental pride? Her teacher?

If Sally cheats (and doesn't get caught and does get her "A") will this really solve her problem? What is Sally's problem?

Suppose Sally decides not to cheat, doesn't do too well on the test and comes out with a "B" and no membership in the Literary Club. Will this reduce the pressure from Mrs. Peters and her mother or increase it? Is the pressure from Mrs. Peters or Sally's mother really the important issue? What is important?

Where does Sally's Christian faith come in? What about Paul's teachings in Philippians 4? What spiritual resources are available? How should Sally use these resources—that is, how should she practice what she has learned from Christ? What are the promised benefits if she will trust Christ in this situation?

WHAT CAN YOU DO?

Take the "GIGO Test" p. 152 to see just where the pressure is coming from in your life and why. If you feel somewhere in the middle of garbage and good, check the three. If you have to honestly admit that you lean toward the garbage side, check one or two, depending on how far you think you're leaning. If you feel that you are in the good area, check the four or the five.

Check over your "check marks" and see how you "print out." If you have a lot of checks in the "somewhere in the middle range" (No. 3) think carefully about just when you seem to lean in the direction of garbage and just when you seem to lean in the direction of good. What are the forces, conditions or events that point you in one direction or the other?

As a specific prayer project, pick a problem area, such as shyness, distrust, feelings of inferiority, etc., and talk to God about this—not just one time or once a week or even once a day. Commit this entire area to God and talk about it constantly with Him. Keep Prov. 3:4–6 in mind: "If you want favor with both God and man, and a reputation for good judgment and common sense, then trust the Lord completely; don't ever trust yourself. In everything you do, put God first, and He will direct you and crown your efforts with success" (*Living Psalms and Proverbs*).

"GIGO TEST"

GARBAGE IN—GARBAGE OUT	1	2	3	4	5	GOOD IN—GOOD OUT
"I am very sensitive and can get my feelings hurt easily when someone criticizes or scolds me."	___	___	___	___	___	"I don't exactly jump for joy when people chop me down but I try not to let it bother me. I simply talk to God about it and tell Him how it is."
"I'm scared to death of my parents and my teachers. I will do just about anything to keep them off my back."	___	___	___	___	___	"I don't always see eye to eye with my parents or teachers, but I usually have respect for them and try to understand them."
"I am basically shy and I have a terrible time making new friends and meeting new people."	___	___	___	___	___	"I'm not exactly the world's greatest extrovert, but I am interested in other people and I do make friends with most people quite easily."
"I often feel very lonely."	___	___	___	___	___	"I never feel lonely. People can let me down but I know I always have Christ."
"I don't have much confidence in myself. I guess I'll always be a failure."	___	___	___	___	___	"I can do just about anything if I want to, with Christ's help."
"Let's face it, people will walk on you if you give them a chance. You've got to stand up for your rights and never trust anybody."	___	___	___	___	___	"I can get along with just about anyone and I try to accept them because I know God has accepted me."

152

". . . obey every law of your government" I Peter 2:13

THE AUTHORITIES: RIGHT OR WRONG?

In the last few years, "disobeying the government" has become the "in" sport or pastime—especially among some under 25. For a small (about 5–7 percent) but loud minority, civil disobedience is more than an idea; it is a way of life. Especially in the United States (but in other countries as well) the government and servants of government —particularly police—have become fair game for social critics of every kind and stripe. Some of this criticism is justified, and some of it is just about as valid as Lucy's protest of "police brutality!" in the cartoon on the next page.

Various explanations are given for the rioting and disruption. Some believe that it's a "communist plot." Others say it's just a new approach to doing what the young have always done—rebel against adult authority. And, there are some who sincerely

believe that the country is in deep trouble and that the "establishment" is rotten and corrupt to the core.

Which explanation is correct? Quite possibly all three have elements of truth in them. But the entire bizarre scene of sit-in demonstrations, campus rioting, the demonstration at the Democratic Convention in 1968, etc., etc., is far too complex a picture to be explained by one simple cause and effect.

The rebellion against "the establishment" affects all of us—and right where we are living. To hear some rebels tell it, we should get rid of all "establishments." Some rebels seem to think that because of governmental graft, corruption, injustice and "overreaction" by husky policemen, all governments must be torn down. What would the rebels put in the place of what they call "corrupt government"? They don't really say; they are too busy screaming their protests which have a continual theme that the establishment is rotten and corrupt, that it must be torn down—and the sooner the better.

Did Biblical writers ever experience anything like what is going on today? Had Peter, Paul, James or John or any of the others who wrote the New Testament ever been "busted" for practically no reason and held incommunicado? Or did they live in some kind of utopia, where the government was perfectly fair, where injustice was nonexistent? It would almost seem that way as you read what Peter had to write to Christian Jews scattered throughout the then-known world. His words almost sound like a public service announcement on being a better citizen . . .

Peter's reasons for "law and order" . . .

"For the Lord's sake, obey every law of your government: those of the king as head of the state, and those of the king's officers, for he has sent them to punish all who do wrong, and to honor those who do right. It is God's will that your good lives should silence those who foolishly condemn the Gospel without knowing what it can do for them, having never experienced its power. You are free from the law, but that doesn't mean you are free to do wrong. Live as those who are free to do only God's will at all times. Show respect for everyone. Love Christians everywhere. Fear God and honor the government" (I Pet. 2:13–17—*Living New Testament, Paraphrased*).

Did Peter "sell out to the establishment"?

The above passage almost sounds as if Peter did indeed "sell out." Why would he urge so strongly that Christians support the government? Throughout history, many governments have proved to be corrupt, dictatorial, tyrannical, and even inhuman. Again and again, governments have corrupted themselves and proven themselves unworthy of support. Many have been overthrown. Many nations have been born in revolution, including the United States of America.

But could it be that the government that was in power at the time that Peter wrote his letter was "more godly" than governments today?

Hardly.

Peter lived under Roman rule. Nero, whom some historians think had severe mental problems, was on Caesar's throne. I Peter is usually dated at A.D. 64, which means that it was written after the great fire in Rome and Nero's first persecution of Christians. Even though Nero revelled in dipping Christians in tar and turning them into living torches for his garden, Peter still said, "Honor the king" (I Pet. 2:17).

Peter isn't the only Biblical writer who talks this way. Paul the apostle had given the same advice to Christians in the church at Rome when he wrote, "Obey the government, for God is the one who has put it there. There is no government anywhere that God has not placed in power" (Rom. 13:1, *Living New Testament*).

Peter and Paul echoed the teachings of Christ as

far as government was concerned. If ever a nation chafed under foreign rule, it was the Jews during the Roman occupation in the first century. Many Jews absolutely refused to pay taxes demanded by Caesar and Christ taught His disciples to pay taxes to Caesar (see Matt. 17:24–27) and to "render unto Caesar the things that are Caesar's and to God the things that are God's" (see Matt. 22:21).

Again and again, the New Testament advises Christians to "submit yourselves to the ordinances of men" (see I Pet. 2:13). How can this be? Does the Bible teach the Christian that he should never question his government or seek to improve it? Many of the campus rebels lump the Scriptures with a "corrupt religious establishment" which they put under the broad term called "the church" and go their merry way preaching revolution for the sake of revolution. But Scripture's teachings on government are based on two important principles that the Christian should be aware of and which he cannot ignore: (1) God has ordained all governments and He allows them to rise and fall according to His permissive will. (2) God has allowed governments for man's own good. As far as the Scriptures are concerned, the term "law and order" is not some "racist cop-out." Law and order are built-in commodities as far as God is concerned because He created the world according to certain natural laws, and He certainly produced an orderly universe. It follows that God wants men to live according to law and order—law and order that produces love, concern, respect among people.

For these reasons, Scripture does teach the Christian to obey the laws of this government and to "honor the king" (or the president, the governor, the mayor, the police chief, the traffic officer, etc.). But this doesn't give any government carte blanc to be tyrannical and terroristic. Governments have responsibilities and are accountable to God. Implied in Scripture's teaching are limitations to just how much honor the government can demand from its citizens, including its Christian citizens. For example, Christ said "Render unto Caesar the things that are Caesar's and unto God the things that are God's." This certainly teaches that there are certain rights and prerogatives that belong to the government and certain rights and prerogatives that do not. It also teaches that God is greater than any government and that the Christian's first allegiance is to God.

One specialist in political science* believes that Scripture teaches that there are four specific areas where the power of the state is limited by God's authority:

1. *The government cannot limit the preaching of the Gospel.* This is why Peter told the Sanhedrin, who had a "court order" from the Roman authorities to make him stop preaching, that he must obey God rather than men (Acts 5:29).

2. *The government cannot demand that the Christian engage in false worship.* The Christians of the first century suffered a great deal of persecution and even more slander, abuse and unpopularity be-

*See "Must We Obey Our Country?" by Walford Petersen, Professor of Political Science, Bethel College, St. Paul, Minnesota, *Eternity* Magazine, March, 1964, p. 28.

cause they refused to worship Caesar. They were perfectly willing to be model citizens in every other way, but they would not knuckle under to the Roman command to worship pagan gods and above all to pay homage to Caesar, who was worshiped as a god.

Not that any Roman citizens really thought that Caesar was a god. The whole idea was part and parcel of the government's propaganda slogans on the "eternal glory and importance of the Roman empire." What the Romans really worshiped was a form of nationalism (which is still around today in many countries).

In the Old Testament, we find Daniel refusing to obey the command of King Darius and for his trouble Daniel wound up in the lions' den. It is significant to recall what Daniel said the next morning when Darius peered over the edge of the pit to view his "remains."

"Hail king, live forever!"

As Peter said centuries later, "Honor the king."

3. *The government is limited in its actions by moral boundaries.* In Romans 13 and I Peter 2, Paul and Peter both point out that governments are established to promote good and repress evil. Christians are admonished to obey the law because if they do so the government will not punish them for doing wrong. But what happens if the government starts doing wrong? What happens when the police become overzealous in enforcing the law? What about the scandal and corruption that has occurred in various police forces and other departments of

government? What happens when a country de-cides that it will "take over" another country or even take over the world with no regard for human rights and the worth of the individual?

Scripture tells us that the baby Jesus was rescued through acts of "civil disobedience." First the wise men "tipped off" Mary and Joseph, who fled into Egypt in direct disobedience to Herod's decree. The baby Moses was another Biblical figure whose life was spared because of civil disobedience. His mother Jochabed tricked the Egyptian government in the classic story, which involved floating Moses down the river in a small cradle made of bulrushes, to be found by Pharoah's daughter herself and reared in the courts of the Egyptians. (See Exod. 1:15–2:4.)

4. *The government cannot overstep its bounds and violate the rights of the church or family.* In other words, according to Scriptures, the govern-ment isn't the only God-ordained institution for man's good. Scripture teaches that the church (Matt. 16:15–18) and the family (Gen. 2:24; and Heb. 13:4) are divinely planned institutions, along with the government (Rom. 13:1). One does not outweigh the other in importance, and that is why separation of church and state is a principle written into the first amendment to the constitution. The church is restricted to its own sphere and it's not al-lowed to dictate decisions and courses of action by the government. At the same time, the state allows the freedom of religion and permits a person to worship according to the dictates of his or her own conscience. As usual, it is a question of balance. Put

the arrangement out of balance—for example the control of government by the church in the Dark Ages, which finally led to the Reformation—and you have problems.

There are plenty of people today who believe that things are "out of balance" more than ever before. Many people, for example, have serious doubts about the "justification for war." For the Christian, the problem becomes compounded when Scripture does not seem to "take sides" in this matter of war. Pacifists have their proof texts and "hawks" seem to have theirs. The answer is not easy for anyone, and the answer must be worked out by each individual according to his own conscience and his own personal relationship to God and Christ.

So when it comes to this matter of "civil disobedience," God seems to "leave us on our own" more than we would like. Scripture gives no cut-and-dried answer, but Scripture does contain a God-ordained, built-in balance that recognizes both sides of the issue. Is civil disobedience ever the right course for the Christian to follow? What each Christian must face is his responsibility to God and to others and just what kind of results his actions will bring.

The following open-end story revolves around an argument between two teen-age boys concerning "police brutality." Justified or not, some teen-agers have the feeling that the policeman is not exactly their best friend. This open-end story, while hypothetical, is based on an actual news event that was broadcast on television.

Police Brutality
Right Before Your Eyes!

Dave and Marv were sitting in Dave's family room watching the tube as a Smothers Brothers rerun was coming to a close. The show had contained a particularly caustic criticism of the "establishment" and as Tommy Smothers signed off, Marv turned to Dave and said: "You know, I think they're right! The adults keep pouring it on us about how we are to behave, but when you look at the corruption and hypocrisy in the establishment you can see that it's all a big joke."

"Now wait a minute, Marv," said Dave. "I think some of the things the Smothers Brothers do are OK, but at times they come through to me as if they have some serious personal hang-ups. They go too far with their criticism of politicians, the army and law enforcement. It's one thing to want to improve things, but it looks to me as if they often take potshots without having any answers of their own to offer."

"Well, you certainly sound like your dad, or the preacher, or somebody has gotten to you," shot back Marv. "What about all the police brutality in these civil rights demonstrations? What about the whole Vietnam mess? What about that Supreme Court justice and all of his little deals on the side that finally forced him to resign? Just the other day I heard my dad talking to one of his friends and bragging about how he had chopped a big chunk out of his income tax payment by a little 'manipulation of certain assets.' "

Dave was about to try to reply to Marv's outburst

when the attention of both boys was refastened on the TV set which had continued on into the "10 o'clock news." The TV news cameras focused on a riot that had occurred that very afternoon at a rock music festival, which had attracted over 100,000 teen-agers. The on-the-spot-coverage zoomed in on a policeman grappling with a long-haired youth in what seemed like physical combat. The youth, outweighed and outmuscled, was backed into a police car with a sickening thud that made it sound like at least three or four bones had been broken. The look on the policeman's face was something less than kindly as he shouted orders to the boy to get in the car and stay there.

"Look at that! LOOK AT THAT!" Marv practically shouted over the TV newscaster's observations. "Exactly what I'm talking about right there in front of you on TV. Who does that cop think he is? He didn't have to rough that kid up that way. All the kid was probably doing was calling him a few names. Man, I don't see how you can stick up for any cop, Dave. They're all a bunch of pigs. Why just last Friday night one of them pulled me over and searched my car for hash. When I asked him why he told me that I looked suspicious and that he was enforcing a new municipal ordinance to crack down on drugs. I don't even use drugs! As far as I'm concerned, they violated my constitutional rights. The whole country is practically down the chute and this thing we just saw on TV proves it!"

Dave had to admit that the police officer had appeared to use a lot more muscle than he needed to and the sound of the kid bouncing off the car had certainly been sickening. He turned to Marv and wondered what he would say . . .

What Should Dave do?

Suppose Dave and Marv are both members of the same youth group at church and both had made decisions for Christ as junior highs. How can Dave "get through" to Marv in a way that shows understanding, but yet helps him see the error in his thinking? What is the error in Marv's thinking?

How does Peter's statement in I Pet. 2:13, "For the Lord's sake, obey every law of the government" apply to this situation?

The Bible teaches the Christian to obey the laws of his government and to show respect for everyone. Is this a practical approach to life in the turbulence of the 1970's? How can a person respect the law if he is a victim of a bonafide case of police brutality or unreasonableness?

WHAT CAN YOU DO?

Use the following "Explore Your Own Feelings" questionnaire to see how you really feel about certain laws under which you must live. If you have no problem with a given area of laws and regulations, you can check 5, which means that you are totally in agreement with obeying these laws for the Lord's sake. If you are not completely in agreement but you still are willing to "go along" you'll probably want to check 4. If you are "not sure" and on the fence (and feeling guilty about it because you think a Christian should never question any laws) check 3. If you are leaning toward the rebellious side, you would check 1 or 2.

Obviously, the "right Christian answer" for all of these is to check 5, which means that you are generally in agreement with all laws and you are obeying them for the Lord's sake.

But this brief quiz is not designed to help you give the "right answers" but to help you think through how you actually feel and why. Be as honest as you can, and after taking the quiz, think through exactly why you have checked certain areas in the way that you have. Where does the balance between "obeying all laws of government for the Lord's sake" and "obeying God and not men" come in?

EXPLORE YOUR OWN FEELINGS

AREA OF CONCERN	CORRUPT, NOT WORTH MY SUPPORT 1	2	NOT SURE— SHOULD BE IMPROVED OR CHANGED 3	OBEY FOR THE LORD'S SAKE 4	5
Traffic laws	—	—	—	—	—
Draft laws	—	—	—	—	—
Curfew laws	—	—	—	—	—
School regulations (dress, hairstyles)	—	—	—	—	—
Civil rights legislation	—	—	—	—	—
Drinking age laws	—	—	—	—	—
Narcotics laws	—	—	—	—	—